Foreign Travelers in America
1810–1935

Foreign Travelers in America
1810–1935

Advisory Editors:

Arthur M. Schlesinger, Jr.
Eugene P. Moehring

AMERICA

A PRACTICAL HANDBOOK

RONALD ELWY MITCHELL

ARNO PRESS

A New York Times Company

New York—1974

Reprint Edition 1974 by Arno Press Inc.

FOREIGN TRAVELERS IN AMERICA, 1810-1935
ISBN for complete set: 0-405-05440-8
See last pages of this volume for titles.

Manufactured in the United States of America

Library of Congress Cataloging in Publication Data

Mitchell, Ronald Elwy, 1905-
    America; a practical handbook.

    (Foreign travelers in America, 1810-1935)
    Reprint of the ed. published by H. Hamilton, London.
    1. United States--Description and travel--1920-
1940. 2. United States--Social life and customs--
1918-1945. I. Title. II. Series.
E169.M65 1974   917.3'04'917   73-13144
ISBN 0-405-05467-X

AMERICA
A Practical Handbook

AMERICA

A PRACTICAL HANDBOOK

By

RONALD ELWY MITCHELL

HAMISH HAMILTON
90 GREAT RUSSELL STREET, W.C.1

First Published - *1935*

134167

PRINTED BY THE STANHOPE PRESS LTD., ROCHESTER, KENT

CONTENTS

INTRODUCTION

THIS book, or collection of six essays on America, is superficial. I was in the country three years, not long enough not to want to write about it after returning to Britain and too long to jot down all my first impressions in an inspired and thorough travel-book. Most of my impressions have simmered into a kind of thick gravy so that what they lack in the brilliance of prejudice they may gain in the lukewarmth of pleasant experience and genuine affection.

I was sent to America by the Commonwealth Fund to study my own pet subject at an American University, to live among the American people and travel over any part of the country I pleased, the idea being that I should know more about America and Americans when I returned to Britain and help in my small way to foster friendly relations between the two great English-speaking nations. My childhood tongue not being English at all but a strange Celtic speech most of which I have since forgotten, I assimilated America much as I assimilated England as a small child twenty years ago, regarding the people as utter strangers at first and then growing into them so firmly with that fatal Celtic adaptability (and superficiality) that I believed myself part of them, until I returned to England in an August gale and knew instinctively as I boarded the London train that I really belonged to none of the three countries but that I liked all three very much, for very different reasons, and that I had gathered a large part of each into my being.

This book is primarily for the English, because the English are the most prejudiced of the four British races against America. This is natural. The English emigrated when it was fashionable to do so, if emigration can ever be quite fashionable, while the Celtic races entered America with their shawls unstylishly tied over their heads and proceeded to plant corn and hack coal and breed nursemaids and police-men and generally make Boston and parts of Pennsylvania what they are to-day.

In Wales, Ireland and Scotland, America is a household word. Cousins, uncles and friends are writing to the old country as they call it, and inviting cautious, untravelled parents to take the risk of their lives and fortunes in a grand visit to the New World. Few of them go, but many dream of going, and the eyes of the races that people the Atlantic verge of Europe are turned west over the water rather than east to their closer, more foreign neighbours.

The Englishman's cousins, uncles and friends are more often in the colonies, and many Englishmen know so little about the American people and their country that even those of education and breeding seem to be unaware that all Americans are not tourists, that there are millions of them who have never crossed the Atlantic, that millions of them are neither wealthy nor destitute, but somewhere in between, like you and me, and that there are beautiful tracts of country in the industrial east as well as modern cities in the romantic west.

The British have much to learn about America, and this book is designed not only for those who have already booked their passage, but for those who are toying with the idea of one day visiting America, and also for those who have no interest in America and no desire to go there, for I was once one of their number.

Around the missionary "hands across the sea" pill I offer plentiful spoonfuls of the jam of practical information and succulent morsels in the form of hints as to how to get the most for your money. America need not be an expensive country to visit, and the Americans themselves are masters in the art of having a good time on a pittance. If they have money, they do not stint themselves, and if they have no money, they still do not stint themselves. They have their faults and their country is by no means perfect, but it is not for the Englishman to judge them until he knows more about them, and the best way to learn is to go there.

"Why do you suppose so many hundreds of thousands of Americans come to Europe? Not more than one out of a hundred Europeans who do go to America ever goes there to learn, to see what we have. And after all, a Woolworth Building or a Ford Plant or a Grand Canyon or a Sharon, Connecticut—and incidentally a mass of 110,000,000 people—might be worth studying. You of all people, Professor, know that most Europeans go to America just to make money. But why are the Americans here? Oh, a few of 'em to get credit for it, back home, or to sell machinery, but most of 'em, bless 'em, come here as meekly as schoolboys, to admire, to learn."

That is from Mr. Sinclair Lewis's "Dodsworth."

Do you know what is meant by "two bits," "European plan," "snatcher," "Yorkville," "five and ten," "Sardi's," "Macy's," "Greenwich Village," "El"?

Do you know how much to tip a New York taxi driver?

Do you know any hotels in the city, or any of its daily papers?

Do you know how much a theatre programme costs in New York?

Do you know where Manhattan Avenue is, where Washington Bridge is, where the Metropolitan Opera House and the Public Library are?

Do you know which is the North River?

If not, read Chapter I.

CHAPTER I

You can go to America and back on an excursion allowing you fifteen days there for about £22 Third Class and £30 or so Tourist Class (United States Line), and £26 15s. on the one class American Merchant Line boats. These do not obtain in the summer season and if you use this cheapest way of crossing you will naturally not see all America in fifteen days, but you could spend a profitable week in New York and a week in the New England countryside, and I personally would do it any time.

There are special tours that take you on a sort of point to point race around the east, starting with New York and leaping to Albany, Niagara, Toronto, Montreal and back to Boston, and so forth, but I have never wasted my time or my money on them. My objection to them is not due to an insane desire to get off the beaten path at all costs. Fifth Avenue has been beaten a long time now and I love it, but if you bring so little imagination to the United States that you can allow yourself to be transported from sight to sight in this humiliating manner, then America cannot fail to be as dull and commonplace as any place you visit, and this book is not for you.

For the usual stay of from three weeks to six months, the round trip fares on the Cunard-White Star Line vary from about £29 to £30 15s. Third Class, £37 15s. to £46 Tourist Class, £48 to £61 Cabin Class and anything up to £88 First Class, and more if you wish.

You must first collect a travelling visa from the American Consulate at 2 Harley Street, London, or from some provincial consulate. They will want to see you, your passport endorsed for America, and a letter from some responsible person or institution stating that your visit is for pleasure, that you do not intend to stay in America indefinitely and that you can afford to support yourself while you are there. They will also want ten dollars or its equivalent from you.

Their great fear is that you will enter the United States and find employment with the intention of settling down there, thereby making one more unemployed American citizen, or alternatively, fail to find employment and become a public charge.

When you pack your clothes for America, you will naturally pack according to season. If it is summer, remember that summer clothes

in America are cheap and good, and that for
rough wear you can buy white duck trousers
for a dollar a pair and for ordinary wear outside New York a linen or Palm Beach suit
from ten dollars up.

If it is winter, remember that American
houses and buildings are steam heated. Thick
English suits are therefore uncomfortable. An
ordinary spring suit or dress will be best for
general wear indoors. You will find thick,
heavy coats and furs very pleasant out of doors.

In England there is little difference between
indoor and outdoor temperatures. In America,
in winter, it may be seventy-five degrees
indoors and twenty below zero outside.

The usual sailing ports are London, Liverpool and Southampton, in reverse order of
importance, and for a reasonable figure you
can possess yourself of, or share, an attractive
small cabin with a porthole, a chair, a radiator,
a wardrobe and a settee, in addition to the
necessities of sleeping and washing.

Soon after the voyage begins there is life-
jacket drill. Novices usually attend and sea-
soned travellers are not to be found. It is
safer and wiser to attend, but you look very
foolish, so you can choose for yourself. Most
people don't look their best in cork and sack-
ing, especially when their faces are wreathed
in self-conscious smiles and their feet are as yet

unaccustomed to the movement of the boat.
Portly old gentlemen stand dutifully at the spot
indicated, and earnest old ladies blanch with
terror when the chief officer gives a brief lec-
ture on taking to the boats.

Your morning bath will probably be hot
salt-water, which feels good but does strange
things to your hair, and stranger things to the
soap, which absolutely refuses to lather. However, a cold fresh-water shower is usually
available.

You will find your appetite increasing as the
days go by. People accustomed to coffee and
toast at ten each morning appear at eight
o'clock and consume orange juice, porridge
and fish, even a chop, followed by griddle
cakes, maple syrup, rolls and butter, marmalade and coffee.

At eleven they eagerly drink their cups of
bouillon and appear promptly for lunch at
12.30 or one o'clock. Then tea at four on deck
or in the promenade lounge. And if there is
a swimming pool on board you swim before
dressing for dinner. After dinner there are
usually moving pictures in the lounge and
dancing afterwards.

You usually hire a chair, with or without
cushions attached, and a rug, at about 7s. 6d.
apiece for the voyage. Your name is attached
to the chair, so that when they reappear in

the morning after being stacked for the night you can recognize your own.

If you are active, you will find little time for sitting, what with deck tennis, shuffleboard, swimming and ping-pong, but if you like reading, there is your chair. And there is usually a library handy if you happen to have come without a book.

As to dressing for dinner on a boat, the following rules may prove useful. In the First Class you always dress. In Cabin Class on a British boat, you dress. On American boats, the majority of Cabin passengers dress on the larger boats, but on the small ones, very few dress. Most people, however, dress for the Captain's dinner.

It is unnecessary to dress in Tourist and Third Class. One or two people occasionally dress in Tourist on the larger boats, but since the purpose of Tourist Class is to make travel inexpensive and informal, it is better not to be fussy.

It is usual not to dress on the first night out, the last night out, and Sundays.

Even if your boat takes only five days to New York, you will find that you settle down completely until that exciting moment when you first see American land.

Unless you are in a great hurry it is pleasant to take a boat that calls at Cherbourg or Cóbh

B—a

and on the other side Halifax or Boston. It is in the nature of a cruise to sail along the north coast of Wales in the early evening with Anglesey grey and misty with a gold edging on Holyhead mountain, and next day to see the green coast of Kerry until the westernmost rocks of Ireland are left behind on the horizon and you are in mid-Atlantic.

After days of water with scarcely a funnel or a furl of smoke, scarcely a fish and scarcely a bird, you suddenly see a little tower standing stiff and erect on the horizon much nearer and clearer than you ever expected for your first sight of another continent.

In a few minutes a long flat piece of coast appears, and if you are heading for Boston this is Cape Cod where the Pilgrim Fathers landed in the *Mayflower* not much more than three hundred years ago.

A few tall chimneys then appear, followed by other spots of land ahead, to the left and to the right. This is Boston Bay you are entering. Soon there is a long coast line ahead, and America is, as it were, all in one piece before you.

I entered this bay on a sunny September afternoon, and against the low green slopes of the coast there were dozens of little white sails. It was a wonderful day, fresh and soft and gentle, and the boat glided smoothly towards the land. The sea was a deep blue with flecks and edges of white foam on it, and the sun was warm and glowing with a late afternoon mildness. It caught the white of the yacht sails and it was as if dozens of butterflies were perched between us and land. As we drew nearer, all the Americans on board became excited and pointed out the buildings to us. Motor boats came flying through the water to greet us, and two aeroplanes whirred over our heads. We stopped at the harbour mouth while the Public Health boat approached and made enquiries, after which we moved slowly in.

Touching the landing stage, it was quite an effort to say "This is America" and feel confidently that this was so. Somehow it looked like most landing stages, and Boston, though it looked unlike any port that I knew, might well have been Glasgow or Hamburg. There was a little knot of people on the quay. They waved and shouted to the Americans on board and we heard some of the stevedores talking their rich Yankee. They looked much the same as those on the Liverpool docks. A car rolled pleasantly along a flat road, and looked safe, somehow, and homely. Beyond one of the sheds a train puffed, with noises not unlike an English train.

After dinner, Boston was lighted, and some of the buildings had electric signs on them. A hotel sign shone above the dark edge of brick and wood, and an advertisement for something in red and white. I meant to look and see what they were whenever I should go to Boston, but once having got the land viewpoint, these beacons were of no interest to me. As I viewed them that evening they were not only the entire city of Boston, but all America, from Patagonia to Alaska.

Much has been written about the approach to New York, so much, indeed, that to start afresh on another description would be in the nature of an anticlimax. You will see it, anyway, unless you are bolting a meal or waiting to pass the immigration officer. This little ceremony generally takes place for aliens just as you are passing the Statue of Liberty and beginning to get the best view of the Skyline. The Customs examination is held on the dockside, immediately after you land.

Treat the immigration and Customs officials with respect. Their work is dull and they have to meet a number of stupid people. And don't believe the people who tell you that they try to make things unpleasant for you. I have entered the States at four different places and three times at New York, and on each occasion both immigration and Customs officials were polite, friendly and speedy.

The minute you land, unless you are being met by friends, you will want to take a taxi to a hotel, and you should know which. Once you are through the Customs, a man will carry your hand luggage (call it baggage in America) to your taxi, and off you go.

By this time coinage should cause you no difficulty. The decimal system makes it simple. A one cent piece is always called a penny, though its value generally hovers near that of the British halfpenny. A five cent piece, usually bearing a buffalo on one side and lo the poor Indian on the other, is called a nickel and serves the purpose a threepenny bit would serve in Britain if it were less easy to lose. Nickels in America are commoner than threepenny bits in South Wales, and that is saying a lot.

A ten cent piece is called a dime. It is smaller than the nickel and looks rather like a sixpence. Its value is about the same, too. In fact the Woolworth's threepenny and sixpenny stores in Britain are "five and ten" stores in America.

A twenty-five cent piece is called a quarter, and in certain areas and by certain people "two bits," though it is a single coin and there is no "one bit."

The terms penny, nickel, dime and quarter are not slang, however, and they refer rather to the coins themselves than to the price of an

article. The distinction is a fine one. You say
"Give me a dime" when you want the coin,
and "Have you got ten cents?" when you want
the amount. If you get it, it comes to the same
thing, but in language there is a difference. If
you ask the young woman in Woolworth's
the price of a piece of soap she will generally
answer "Ten cents." Listen for this distinction. Most Americans are unaware that they
make any. I do not know how local this tendency is, but I do know that it is dangerous to
make linguistic generalisations for America.
After a few weeks in New England I became
accustomed to the term "Pardon me" and
used it as often as I used "Excuse me." I
jumped to the hasty conclusion that "Pardon
me" was the American for "Excuse me." Well,
it is, in some places. But I visited Pennsylvania
and said "Pardon me" once, and there were
little, appreciative cries of delight. "How
English" they chanted, "we always say 'Excuse
me'."

You can reckon the quarter as being worth a
shilling or thereabouts. It is the coin you
usually give a porter for the average piece of
work he does for you. A fifty cent piece may be
called half a dollar, but is generally just fifty
cents.

A dollar is a coin in the West and parts of
the Middle West, a silver coin of the cartwheel

variety, but in the east it is a bill, never a note. In slang a dollar is a buck, but this term refers to price more frequently than to the actual coin, and it is usual to say that a dinner set you back three bucks, though in polite society a dollar is just a dollar. And in all societies, polite or otherwise, a dollar is worth what the exchange tells you, generally a little over four shillings.

There are two-dollar bills, five-dollar bills, ten-dollar bills and twenty-dollar bills, and if you are wisely carrying travellers' cheques with you (travelers' checks in America) you will not have to bother with the higher denominations.

Now for taxis. The regulation fare is fifteen cents for the first quarter of a mile and five cents for each succeeding quarter of a mile; thus a mile costs you thirty cents, two miles fifty cents, three miles seventy cents, and so on. And Manhattan being over twenty square miles in area you can run up to quite a number of dollars. Not that the taxis stay on Manhattan island. They will cross the bridges into other boroughs if you want them to. In fact, I suppose you could taxi all the way out to California if you wished, but it would cost you six hundred dollars in fare alone, and I think you would have to do something about the driver's bed. You would also have a job persuading him.   He would probably drive you a dozen blocks to the nearest mental hospital. Anyhow, the train is much cheaper and more comfortable.

You pay a little extra for waits and for heavy baggage and, as in England, you tip the driver. Ten cents is sufficient for a brief journey, fifteen cents for a moderate journey and a quarter for a four-mile journey.

Use only the taxis that show the fare on them in large letters on the side, and refuse all taxis that show a different price scale from the 15 cent-5 cent scale.

Inside a New York taxi you will see a small photograph of the taxi driver on his licence, which is displayed for your benefit. You are supposed to inform the police if the photograph and the man are clearly different and you are also supposed to note his name and number. As a rule you forget unless you are a nervous character.   Not that the names lack a striking quality.   Some of them may be Doyles and Nolans, but as often as not, the taxi drivers of New York would seem to have sprung from Moscow, Athens, Naples, Warsaw and Berlin.

As for hotels, they are a complicated business, and since you will probably have to use them not only in New York but all over the States, we may as well dispense with them now.

It matters comparatively little to which

hotel you are driven when you first arrive, provided that it is comfortable and within your means. After one night or so you can decide whether you want to stay put or whether some other hotel would suit your purpose or your purse, or both, better. As soon as you arrive in your New York hotel, look up the standard Hotel Guide, which you will find side by side with a Gideon Bible and several packs of telegraph blanks in the bureau drawer. If you are in some anxiety as to how to make your money last out the full length of your stay, note down the hotels within your price range. If you do not have to do this, so much the better, but it is good, anyway, to see this guide and on payment of fifty cents to possess a copy. Even if your aim is not to secure good, low-priced accommodation, it sometimes happens that you wish to know how many and what scale of hotels are in some particular city at which you may arrive at night, and it is easier for both you and the taxi driver if you know exactly where you want to go, even in a city you have never seen in your life before.

To come back to your first night in New York, if you are willing to pay a fairly high price for a first class hotel, there are the famous Biltmore, Waldorf Astoria, Sherry Netherland, Ritz Carlton, Plaza, Savoy Plaza, Pierre and

Saint Regis. There are also the Gotham and the Drake.

If you want a medium-priced hotel, there are the Algonquin, New Yorker, Pennsylvania, Park Central, Paramount, Barbizon Plaza, Saint Moritz, Roosevelt and Shelton.

If you want to make your money go as far as you can, there are the Lincoln, Taft, Tudor, Knickerbocker and Bristol.

There are cheaper hotels yet and you will find them in the Hotel Guide. If you possibly can, don't stint yourself for the first two or three days in New York. It is an expensive city, but well worth it.

I have stayed in most of the above hotels except the most expensive ones, which I classify on hearsay. And as far as hotels go, hearsay isn't far wrong.

Hotels would easily fill a book in themselves. In the great cities they generally fall into classes, the palatial ones, the quiet aristocratic ones, the glittering medium-priced ones, the quiet cheap ones, the moth-eaten cheap ones, the inferior expensive ones, the noisy travelling salesmen ones, and in fact any other class you can think of. It is good to stay in one of each kind, and then decide which you like best.

You should know all about the European and American plans in hotels. You will occasionally find the American plan working

in America, but not often.   European plan
means that you pay for your room or room and
bath alone and for no meals.   This is the most
common method, especially in cities.   You
can take your meals in the hotel dining-room
or in the grill-room if it has one, or least expen-
sively in the coffee-shop attached, or if you like
at some establishment not connected with the
hotel at all.   This arrangement leaves you perfectly free, and since you may arrive at an
American hotel at any time of the day you
please, and leave at any time up to six o'clock
in the evening without anyone showing any
tendencies to want to make you pay double,
the American plan has its points and in this
particular might well be popularized in Europe.

Some hotels, like the Barbizon Plaza, push
a small breakfast through the door by way of
a gift from the management, but Bed and
Breakfast as such are not well known in
America.

As for the bathroom, most modern hotels
have a small tiled bathroom with tub and
shower attached to every room, and the price
stated includes this.   Many hotels quote a price
for rooms without bath, and a price, usually
fifty cents a day more, for a room with a bath.
If you take a room without a bath, you can
generally find a bathroom a little way along
the passage, just as in the average British hotel,

but, as also in the average British hotel, you may find the bathroom occupied, and Americans cannot bear to wait, and you will doubtless find that you, when in America, cannot bear to wait either.

Most double rooms are twin bedded and you can often get a double room with bath attached for four dollars where you would have to pay two dollars and fifty cents single.

A good average to work on is from two dollars to four dollars a night for a single room without bath, and 2.50 to 4.50 with bath. Twin-bedded rooms in the same scale would run from 3.50 without bath to eight dollars with bath.

Your breakfast will cost you twenty-five cents in a drugstore and fifty cents or a dollar in a hotel. Your lunches vary from thirty-five cents to a dollar, rarely more and rarely less. For thirty-five cents a city restaurant will give you fruit juice, a salad or a sandwich and a cup of coffee. In summer that is all very well. In winter, fifty cents will buy you soup, entrée or roast, pie or ice cream, and coffee or milk. Sixty-five cents will see a salad edging its way between your roast and your pie. Seventy-five cent lunches are quite lavish and as much as anyone from Britain need eat, with tea only three hours and a half ahead.

Dinner may cost only twenty-five cents in a

southern village, fifty cents in a small town,
seventy-five or eighty-five cents in the average
restaurant and so on up to ten dollars if you
choose the right wines. Not that you can't go
beyond ten dollars. You can. But if you are
hard up, a dollar should be your limit.

In your hotel room there will be a telephone.
If every penny counts, go to the telephone
booths downstairs in the lobby and your call
will cost you five cents. If you ask the girl in
the lobby who will put you through with no
inconvenience on your part, you pay ten cents.
The numbers are higher than in Britain, consisting of an exchange name and five figures,
the first figure being constant for the exchange
name, but not confined to one exchange only.
In the booths you may use telephones with
dials attached or without dials. It is the custom
to drop a nickel in the slot to call the exchange.

If you want to write a letter or postcard,
remember that you can buy stamps at other
places than post offices. Your hotel may sell
them to you at the cigar stand or there will be
a machine. Unlike British stamp machines,
you pay a trifle more for your stamps if you get
them this way.

The Inland postage is one cent for a postcard and three cents for a letter. Abroad, you
must attach a five cent stamp. If you write

very thick letters you had better have them weighed.

American stamps are constantly commemorating occasions and institutions. However, whether the stamp is small and shows merely a President's face on it or whether it is large and displays a National Park, the colours remain the same, green for one cent, red for two cents, mauve for three cents and blue for five cents.

Washington (George) used to be depicted on all the smaller denominations, but recently, Franklin has taken possession of the one cent stamp and Theodore Roosevelt of the five cent stamp, leaving Washington with the two cent and three cent stamps. After all, he was their *first* President. Lincoln and others are represented, too, but you don't use them every day of your life.

Down in the lobby of your hotel you can buy newspapers, but if you are a stickler for an odd penny here and there, buy your paper outside in a store or off a stand where you are charged the proper price for it and no more. Hotels usually charge you more, on the assumption that if you can afford to stay in a room with a bed in it, a penny or two more won't break you.

Some hotels, however, instead of charging you more for your paper than they should, give you one or even two newspapers each morning as a greeting from the management. That makes you wonder how much the hotels that charge you extra make. However, it costs a few cents to run the elevator up to the seventeenth floor and down, so be thankful that they don't charge you a nickel for that trip.

Remember that papers bought some distance out of their home towns are a penny or two more. You will generally find the regulation prices marked at the top of the front page.

The two chief daily papers of New York are the *New York Times* (democratic) and the *New York Herald Tribune* (republican). They are each two cents a copy on week days and ten cents a copy on Sundays. But on Sundays you get such a magnificent collection of reading and pictorial matter that if you have to miss your paper on weekdays you should never miss it on Sundays.

It is said that a Sunday edition of the New York Times once fell out of an aeroplane and stunned a cow. When you have bought your first copy you will wonder why the cow wasn't killed outright.

If you are interested in journalism you will know the other daily papers already. Even if journalism leaves you cold you might buy a tabloid, that is to say, a sensational and insensitive journal the perusal of which will, the editors hope, thrill you and at the same time, though the editors do not know this, show you to what the American language can come.

If you go to the news stand in the centre of Times Square, you will see papers from all parts of the United States. This is where Westerners and Southerners and Mid-Westerners get the news of the old home town.

Moreover, for the New Yorkers who were born or whose parents or grandparents were born in Sweden or Greece or Italy or Spain, or Russia or Hungary, there are papers written in the languages of those countries.

As for magazines, you will find at the book stands of your hotel or of the great terminal stations the equivalents of the British magazines on any subject which interests you. For general reading there are *Scribner's*, *Harper's* and the *Atlantic Monthly*, and you may become a current history addict. There are motoring, theatrical, athletic, business, boating, flying, photographic, domestic and story magazines of all kinds. You can generally tell what a magazine is like from its cover. The sober ones have sober covers and the wild west stories and love romances do not hide their light under a bushel. Magazines are about the most honest and hidebound things out. For a democratic country, they stick to their classes with an almost feudal tenacity.

There are some excellent bookstores in New

York, some connected with the larger publishing houses, some not. There is also a large number of small bookstores especially around Times Square and on Sixth Avenue, Seventh Avenue and Broadway in the Forties. These stores specialize in cheap books and mildly pornographic reprints done up in nice editions. You can sometimes buy very good bargains in these stores. At all events you can look around.

Books will seem expensive. A novel costing seven and sixpence in Britain will appear in America costing 2.50, a little over ten shillings. You will not find the many series of inexpensive books of the kind that line a modest library in Britain. You can, of course, buy the Everyman editions there at rather more than you pay for them in Britain, and you will see other familiar libraries advertised.

For ninety-five cents a copy, however, you can buy the books of the Modern Library, neat, attractive little volumes constantly increasing in number and including such authors as Balzac, James Branch Cabell, d'Annunzio, Dostoyevsky, Dreiser, Anatole France, Ibsen, James Joyce, D. H. Lawrence, Maupassant, Merejkowski, Poe, Proust, Schnitzler, Turgenev, Oscar Wilde and Thornton Wilder.

A good thing to do upon arrival in New York is to buy a map of it, unless you already have one or are given one by your hotel.

c—a

You will see that as far as you are concerned New York is the Borough and Island of Manhattan. You will also see how it happens that this island is surrounded by the water of three rivers, the Hudson, the East, and the Harlem. Until you have looked at a map you will be very vague about this.

New York is a simple city to find your way in. In all but the southernmost section of the island, the avenues run north and south, and the streets east and west, and they are numbered, First Avenue being on the east side of the city and First Street in the South, two miles from Battery Park, the tip of the island.

Fifth Avenue divides the city, all streets west of Fifth Avenue having West preceding their number, and all streets east of Fifth Avenue having East preceding their number.

The island comes to a point at its north-west end at West 220th Street, the East Side virtually coming to an end at East 138th Street, where the Madison Avenue Bridge takes you over the Harlem River into the Bronx.

Broadway runs slantwise across the main part of the city, upsetting the square pattern of everything. It is at 9th Street that it starts doing this and every time it crosses an avenue it makes a set of crossroads and these all have names. It starts by almost running into Fourth Avenue at 14th Street and this is called Union

Square. At Fifth Avenue and 23rd Street it crosses again at Madison Square, at Sixth Avenue and Thirty-fourth Street there is Greeley Square, at Seventh Avenue and 42nd it runs into Times Square and stays in Times Square for three or four blocks, pursuing its north-westerly course to Eighth Avenue and 59th Street at Columbus Circle and so on north into the Bronx.

The Avenues numbering from one to twelve are easy and regular except in one place. Remember that Fourth Avenue becomes Park Avenue quite early in its northerly career and remains Park Avenue even into the Bronx. Between Third and Park is Lexington Avenue, which you can remember as $3\frac{1}{2}$ Avenue if that makes it any easier, and between Park and Fifth there is Madison Avenue, which you can call $4\frac{1}{2}$. No one I ever heard uses these terms, but during the first confused days they helped me to remember which came where.

There is a bit of a Thirteenth Avenue here and there, and between 1st and 26th Streets on the East Side there are three extra avenues, Avenue C, Avenue B and Avenue A, if we are to adhere to the east-west numbering.

Central Park occupies a long rectangle in the northern half of Manhattan, being three avenue blocks wide (about half a mile) and fifty-one street blocks long (about two miles and a half). It is all just west of Fifth Avenue; in fact, Fifth Avenue runs along the east margin of the Park just as Park Lane in London runs along the east margin of Hyde Park.

In the northern part of Manhattan, some of the avenues take other names.

Eighth Avenue becomes Central Park West between 59th and 110th Streets and then becomes Eighth Avenue again. Sixth Avenue comes to a stop against Central Park South (59th Street) and when it sprouts again at 110th Street it is called Lenox Avenue.

Ninth Avenue becomes Columbus Avenue at 59th Street and then loses itself in Morningside Drive.

At 100th Street an entirely new avenue called appropriately Manhattan Avenue springs up between Eighth (now Central Park West) and Ninth (now Columbus). Manhattan Avenue continues for about thirty blocks and then becomes Saint Nicholas Avenue.

Tenth Avenue becomes Amsterdam Avenue at 59th Street and soberly remains Amsterdam almost until it reaches the Harlem River. Then for some reason it hysterically disappears, finds itself again for a block or two, frantically calls itself Tenth again and runs into Broadway.

Eleventh Avenue becomes West End Avenue at 59th Street and runs into Broadway at 106th.

Twelfth Avenue is somewhat put out of countenance by Riverside Drive. If it had been content to stop at 59th like some of the other avenues, it might have been taken for the splendid Riverside Drive itself, which begins at 72nd and winds graciously along and overlooking the Hudson River. But no. Between 130th and 157th Streets, after not appearing for some sixty or seventy blocks, it suddenly tries to stage a come-back side by side with Riverside Drive. It fails, of course, except for those seventeen blocks.

Now that you are in New York City and can find your way about, what are you to do and where are you to go in it? That is so much a matter of personal taste, and taste or no taste, there is so very much you can do in New York that the wisest thing for me to do is to state simply what I should do if I were given a week in it, or rather what I should plan to do, for the minute I set my foot in New York, I should instantly start doing something else. New York is like that.

I would use most of the known means of transport, bus, subway, elevated, street car and taxi, I would walk along Broadway, Park Avenue, Fifth Avenue, 42nd Street and 57th Street. I would ride in Central Park and along Riverside Drive, I would step inside the Grand Central Terminal and the Pennsylvania Station. I would go to the top of the Empire State Building, I would eat at a variety of places, a Greenwich Village inn, a Sixth Avenue delicatessen, a French restaurant, a German restaurant and several plain and good American restaurants. I would go to the Metropolitan Opera if the season were on and find out what music, if any, was to be heard at Carnegie Hall and elsewhere. I would go to a play or two, I would go inside Saint Patrick's Cathedral and the Metropolitan Museum of Art and several department stores. I would walk through some of the foreign sections, and indeed walk around the town generally and look at the people.

Did I say a week? Oh well, if you like, you can take a bus that will show you all New York in a day for the equivalent of thirty shillings, or you can live there until you die on your hundredth birthday and still you won't have seen it all.

You can ride anywhere and any distance on the Subway (underground railway) for a nickel. You just slip your nickel into a machine and push your way through a turnstile and you can go as far as the line will take you without further payment. The Subway is ugly and dirty compared with the neat and colourful London tube, and the stations have little charm. The trains, however, are speedy and cheap and if you are interested in people you will see a variety of types and characters on the Subway, especially during the business hours. Familiarize yourself with the various lines, which any map will explain more simply than words and remember that there are expresses and locals, the expresses skipping the less important stations.

The Subway occasionally comes out of the ground and is then much the same thing to look at or to ride in as the Elevated or El or "L" which also runs in its own right along various avenues and streets and sometimes among backyards, supported by iron pillars and iron framework of a practical but harsh and unlovely design. The dockside railway at Liverpool closely resembles the New York El and must frequently startle the New Yorker who has come to "this blessed plot, this earth, this realm, this England" in order to escape from the shrieking Sixth Avenue trains and streets filled with ironwork.

You put your nickel in the slot for the El just as you do for the Subway, but you walk up steps instead of down them. No elevators (or lifts) take you up, and in the Subway no elevators take you down. Like the District Railway along the London Embankment, the tunnel is close to the surface. I remember coming up in an elevator at a Brooklyn Subway station, but I cannot recall such a station on Manhattan.

You see more for your nickel on the El. In fact a long ride on it is something like a scenic railway doing the seamier side of the city, for naturally the "ritzy" streets do not have electric trains crashing down their middle every two or three minutes, and rentals are lower for private property overlooking (and overhearing) the railroad. You cannot see much of the street when you are in the centre of it twenty or more feet above ground level, but you can see the sidewalk on one side and you have an excellent view of the second floor windows. At this juncture it might be well to state that the ground floor in Britain is the first floor in America and so on. If the Empire State Building were carried over to London and planted here, its 102nd floor would be the 101st which, from the point of view of record breaking, would be a pity.

Sometimes the El takes you right behind the huge tenement buildings, and if you are vulgarly curious you can see negroes reading their newspapers, Italians eating, Slavs working and Americans talking. This state of affairs is occasionally shuffled around and you see the Americans eating and the Italians talking.

The Subway and the El are very much in the life and blood of New York City. It is significant that two plays of New York life are called "Subway" (Elmer Rice) and "L," a one-act play by Leopold Atlas.

Trams in America are called trolley cars, surface cars or street cars, the usage differing in different localities. They are less exciting and interesting than other means of travel, especially in New York, but if you want to trundle down town or up town and you have plenty of time to spare, it will cost you just a nickel. In other cities you may have to pay a dime on a trolley car, but in other cities the trolley car may be the only means of getting where you want. In many places in the eastern States, trolley cars are going out of fashion and the lines are being uprooted. You can see the scars of the one-time trolley tracks in many a New England small town where they were once such popular vehicles of transport, and early this year the last street car clattered its way down Madison Avenue in New York City. That is only one of the many street car services in New York, and there are many left, but it looks like the beginning of the end. Private cars have been largely instrumental in ousting the trolley car, and buses have helped. With one automobile to every three people in the United States trolley cars with their clumsy rattling are only for the poor.

The Fifth Avenue coach (euphemism for

bus) costs a dime if you go one block only and a dime if you go all the way. The conductor holds a little machine in front of you and you unhesitatingly slip your dime into the aperture. You never hand the dime to him. If you have no dime, you hand him what you have and he will give you change. He will never put your dime in the snatcher for you. Your change comes all complete, containing at least one dime, which you then solemnly insert. If you don't want the ride on a Fifth Avenue bus, it's worth while going on one just for the ritual, especially if you think America deficient in ritual.

After the luxury of London buses you will find the Fifth Avenue coach a prehistoric little object with no room for your knees, reminiscent of the things that trundled along Oxford Street some twenty years ago if you are old enough to remember them. However, the moment you think of laughing at them, take a look at the elegant taxis and remember the queer little boxes on wheels that still run around London.

Choose a sunny morning on which to view the whole of Fifth Avenue from the top of one of these buses. There are so many traffic jams that you can see everything there is to be seen, and if you take the Number 5 bus north you can swing westwards to the winding glories of Riverside Drive, and if you choose a mild evening you can go on and on along the Hudson River with the lights of Jersey Side twinkling opposite and an occasional barge glowing with tiny lights.

If you are staying at a hotel overlooking Central Park South (and the Saint Moritz is one of these) you will spend a good deal of time just looking out of your window. Central Park from a high window is a lovely sight at any time, but most especially in the fading light of a late September or early October afternoon with the late trees just beginning to turn brown and yellow, and the water shining in the lake. And when the spring comes you will say that this is surely lovelier than the fall, and so on with every season and every month.

If you look even just once, you will notice the buggies standing patiently in the street and waiting to take you for a ride. If you have any soul at all it will not be long before you succumb.

I use "buggy" as a generic term for any horse-drawn vehicle. This is very "hick" of me, I know, but as a product of the automobile age I am not familiar with the names of the different kinds of carriages, open or closed, believing rather obstinately that such information, like a knowledge of wines, should grow with you and not be vulgarly mugged up out of an encyclopedia afterwards.

However young and frivolous you may be, or elderly and bashful, you will after your first five minutes in a buggy be very dignified and completely at your ease. There is something about the steady jogging movement and the satisfying cloppety clop of the horse and the snap of the whip that makes you utterly impervious to the vulgar people who look down from Fifth Avenue buses with surprise when they see that you are not an old lady wearing black watered silk and a gold chain, and the nasty modern, mechanical children of a prosaic age who will occasionally jeer as you come to a gentle standstill at a stoplight.

You will choose a sunny afternoon, of course, and you will be able to admire the buildings as you ride. Generally, unless you are on a bus, you go so fast in New York that when you ask "What's that place?" your companion's answer comes a block later, and if he is a New Yorker he never knows anyway. Admittedly, your chief thrill is the leisured trot and its complete contrast with the gliding swiftness of the modern automobile. If you are forty or fifty you will have other emotions, but they are a closed book to those who are not yet thirty.

You should go up the Empire State Building, not because it is a thing that every foreign tourist is expected to do, but because what you see from the Observation Tower is so breath-

takingly beautiful that only the most sated and
blasé creatures can despise it. Go in the afternoon on a clear day in the spring or fall, have
tea if you like in the café on the eighty-sixth
floor, and stay up the building until it grows
dark so that you can watch the city being
lighted. On other occasions you can go in the
morning or at night, but your first visit should
take in this incomparable sight; below you is
the whole island of Manhattan. The blunt
end of the island, so familiar to you if you have
studied the map, is there to the south beyond
the downtown group of skyscrapers. The East
River is on one side of you and the Hudson on
the other. There are boats out in the harbour,
boats on both rivers, and boats cooped up in
the docks, looking like toys. The automobiles
creep along Fifth Avenue like a long line of
blackbeetles, and the people swarm like ants.
When it is growing dark, each street and
avenue spurts rows of tiny yellow lights, criss-
cross in perfect pattern, with Broadway breaking up the square design with its slant and the
evenness of the lighting with its glare. The New
Jersey coast is dotted with lights as far as you
can see, and all the Hudson and East River
boats that carry crowds of working men and
women back to their suburban homes glitter
as they cross and re-cross like something in a
fairy tale. It is all so fantastic, this beauty on

ugliness, this charm cheek by jowl with squalor. Down in the city, the tenements are deadly and miserable, the streets untidy, the cars and buses dull and dirty, the Subway noisy and ugly. The El rattles its cheap and flashy way down Sixth Avenue and the streets are grey with dust. And from this, like a fresh green bulb of hyacinth growing out of a muck heap, gleams the white and silver of the Empire State Building, clean and strong and beautiful, and from its remoteness the grime and noise below fade into a rumbling haze, and the whole thing looks good and lovely.

New York grows on you. If you dislike it on your first visit or even your second, you will begin to sense a certain fascination when you know the city a little better. At first it is all bewildering, and the squalor impresses you more than anything else. Later, you will cease to notice the squalor, but the awe and wonder still remain, tempered with a friendly feeling of familiarity. The people are still hard of face, but interesting. You can watch them coming out of the Subway at five o'clock and indeed all the evening; you can see them sitting in rows tightly wedged or strap-hanging on their way to the Bronx or Brooklyn or Queen's. They are more Italian than a London crowd, and rather more Jewish as well. Most of the Subway crowds look tired and pale, and many of the men are of the dark, scrubby type, that look dirty and unshaven every evening. Some of them will be reading Jewish or Italian newspapers.

Drop into a typical Broadway drugstore. It need not be on Broadway to be typical. There you can watch more people and at the same time drink coffee and eat cream cheese and olive sandwiches, three-deckers toasted—fifteen cents extra. Most drugstores have collections of books, many of little value, but you can sometimes pick up some good bargains in cheap new copies of books, notably classics, and especially classics with a faintly erotic appeal.

You will not, however, want to eat exclusively at drugstores and if you are very British, you may never want to eat at drugstores at all, or cafeterias, or automats. They must be very dull for the Americans who have always had them and who cannot afford anything better, and if you are feeling sad and reflective, you had better avoid them, or you will see just a blank row of dull human animals, hastily refuelling themselves so that they can exist for a few more hours without feeling the pangs of hunger. There they are, some of the men wearing hats, some of the women without hats, eating un- attractive food unattractively in an unattrac- tive place. If you have only just arrived in

New York and have not often eaten at the equivalent of these places in London, you may enjoy them. I did. The standard of the food is higher than in similar restaurants in England. The coffee may not be of the best and the pie may be a little leathery, but on the whole, cheap food in such places is not bad, and sometimes it is really good.

Drugstores serve only the simplest food, sandwiches, coffee, and ice cream, no more, but you can choose your meal at a cafeteria from an entire exhibition of food. You take your tray and a little parcel consisting of knife, fork and spoon at one end and gather your meal as you follow the line. Some cafeterias put up a notice saying: "It is not discourteous to pass others in line," meaning that if you want orange juice and salad, you can pass the woman who is debating over soup and lamb chops without feeling embarrassed. Other cafeterias make it impossible to pass the leisurely ones unless you creep between the metal rails or climb over their backs, and this would definitely be considered discourteous. In a cafeteria you generally pay at the end of the line before you eat. Then you hurry to a table and eat your soup and drink your coffee before they are quite cold. In cafeterias and other cheap restaurants, always look to see whether there is a ticket machine imme-

diately inside the door. If there is, pull out
the ticket and hand it to the girl who checks
your food in a cafeteria or brings you your
tray in a restaurant, and she will punch it
opposite the cost of your meal. As you go out
you pay at the desk.

Automats are interesting—once. They are
singularly impersonal places, but if you are
prejudiced against them by reason of childish
memories of stale chocolate and damp or very
dry biscuits obtained from British railway
station machines, it is only fair to state that the
food in the New York automat is fresh. There
is a certain fascination about holding a glass
beneath a silver tap, inserting your dime and
watching the milk pour smoothly out until
you think it is going to spill. But no. At the
very last moment the stream is suddenly
dammed and there you are with a full glass of
milk in your hand—that is if you want a glass
of milk.

As for places to eat with some individuality
to them, books have been written on the subject, and it is not a bad idea to have a book on
New York restaurants, especially the intimate,
friendly kind that tells you the prices and the
specialties (specialities in English). But be
sure that the book is a recent publication.
Restaurants come and go in New York with
dismaying rapidity, and it is risky to make

D—a

any definite statements without first-hand, red-hot information.

There are the hotels, ranging from the very best and most expensive to the dullest and cheapest, and there are the restaurants, some unashamedly American and some beguilingly foreign. The fashionable and attractive foreign restaurants will be mentioned in books on New York restaurants and occasionally advertised in papers; the unfashionable ones are almost entirely patronized by the foreigners for whom they were intended and you must find them for yourself, if you are of an adventurous spirit.

You can combine this search for interesting foreign restaurants with slumming all over Manhattan. The most famous foreign communities are either down town or up town, so if you are staying in the theatre district you will have to make a definite excursion to them. Once you are down on the Bowery, which you want to see anyway, you are within walking distance of the chief New York Ghetto, the Italian quarter and Chinatown. The Ghetto is mostly east of the Bowery, the Italian quarter is south of Washington Square, and China-town south of it by some half dozen blocks.

Bowery is the core, as it were, of these three districts, and Bowery is the down town name for Fourth Avenue, which, higher up, we know as the ultra fashionable Park Avenue. It is obvious what these quarters can supply you with in the way of food, but unless you are adventurous, you had better be guided in these districts. Bowery is famous in song and the Five Points (or Five Pernts if you prefer) in legend.

North-east of this section, with Second Avenue as a core and running up as high as 15th or 16th Street, you can find a section devoted to a mixture of races, including Russians, Hungarians, Roumanians, Bulgarians, Armenians and Greeks, a sprinkling of some and a Hebraic flavour to most. If you happen to be there, some of the store-keepers will recommend you places to eat. It is usually wiser in New York never to ask for recommendations from total strangers, but I found the down town business men very polite and helpful in this respect.

Up town, with Lenox Avenue as a core, there is Harlem, the negro quarter, but Harlem is uninteresting during the day, and at night it is better not to slum at all. Harlem is full of well-known night clubs and your book or a friend or your hotel will tell you all about them.

Along the best-known part of Broadway in the theatre district are any number of Chinese restaurants, not as Chinese as the Chinatown ones, but Chinese enough. You can look at a dull cabaret and see rather commonplace New

Yorkers trying to be exotic and daring and not succeeding very well. You can eat tolerably good American or Chinese food, and you can dance on a floor that permits of only tiny paces if you are not to fall into the tables that crowd the edges. If you are lucky you will have a sharp-witted little Chinese waiter who will talk to you about England, which he has never seen but hopes to when he has saved enough money to go there. If he is the same one I talked to, he will praise Milton and Shakespeare to you, and if you dare to mention Dante or Goethe his Oriental lip will curl with scorn as he sets down your soup and tells you once and for all that England has the best poets and that no one else is in the running.

If you are very lucky, or unlucky, whichever way you look at it, you find a drunken, brawling crowd instead of the dull suburban one. After their behaviour on the dance floor the naughty cabaret will resemble an English parish concert. Once when I was in one of these places, a woman attracted much attention by falling to the floor, groaning, and calling upon God to help her. Among her companions she caused some commotion, but the Chinese waiters looked as if they were accustomed to that sort of thing and continued to serve their quieter customers quite unperturbed. Possibly they were all thinking of England and murmuring Paradise Lost to themselves, though I hardly think our friend was typical of the New York Chinese waiter. They did, however, seem to possess a quiet dignity and aloofness which the noisy Americans were far from possessing. However, it is scarcely fair to judge. These same Americans probably conducted their day's work with the bored resignation that often amounts to something resembling dignity and detachment. I have always had my suspicions of inscrutability. It is so frequently to be found associated with a low standard of intelligence.

Lexington Avenue way, among the eighties, is called Yorkville and is a German and Bavarian section. Here you can eat German food and drink beer while waiters clad in mountain costume sing songs to you. And if you go there at Christmas time the roast gosling is very good.

If you are slumming rather than gormandizing, you will come across a little Irish colony about ten blocks north of Yorkville. Gloomy little restaurants with aspidistras in the window will remind you of that section of Dublin north of the Liffey of which the more sordid Irish novelists are so fond. Unless you are very tough indeed you will not want to eat here. Nor will you be much attracted by the Spanish Cuban quarter fourteen or fifteen blocks north

of this little Erin.   The streets are dark and
furtive, but here and there is a blaze of lights,
blaring with tangos and rumbas, flashy wenches
in scarlet and yellow, and lean, brown young
men with sideburns.   This little colony is
perched around the north-east corner of Central Park, and its core is not a street but a
crashing and passionate little movie theatre
at the corner of 110th Street and Fifth Avenue.

There are other foreign sections in plenty,
but these should be enough to take at second
hand.

A quarter which can hardly be called foreign
but which you should treat as such is Greenwich Village.   It is supposedly New York's
Bohemian section, but it is not what it was.
Nor, indeed, is anywhere in New York, so this
is no particular distinction.   You may happen
to meet peculiar people even in these days in
Greenwich Village, most of them having pre-
tentions of some sort to literature, art or music.
Some of them may have talent, but as a rule
the talented ones do not look Greenwich
Villagy and some of them do not live there at
all.   You will find Greenwich Village down
beyond Washington Square, the streets between
4th and 9th just west of Fifth Avenue, together
with Sheridan Square, McDougal Street and
Christopher Street being the centre of the
district.

If you neither want to eat at a hotel nor in a cheap joint nor in a remote quarter of the city, you can get excellent food in well-known places near the chief hotels, with both American and a foreign flavour.

To mention just a few, there is the famous Lobster on West 45th Street for sea food, Roth's Grill and the Brass Rail on Seventh Avenue, almost in Times Square and quite handy for theatres, and there is Sardi's, which is famous for its caricatures, its food, and its clientele. Sardi's is Italian and on West 44th Street, almost in your theatre lobby.

The Blue Ribbon, also on West 44th Street, is the best thing in German food, and if you like pig's knuckle and sauerkraut with beer, followed by apfel strudel, you should not miss the Blue Ribbon.

For French food there is the charming and quiet Maison A. De Winter on West 48th Street with its hors d'œuvres and drawing-room atmosphere. There is also a less quiet, but really inexpensive restaurant called Pirolle's on West 45th Street. It is quite a useful place to know.

The Chalet Suisse, on West 52nd Street, is somewhat out of the Times Square district, but is pleasant for lunch. The theatre district is plentifully besprinkled with small German and Italian restaurants, some of them good, some of them poor.

If you feel adventurous, try something at the
Chili Villa on West 49th Street. It is Mexican
and so decorated that you feel hot the minute
you enter. Go in winter if you are cold and go
in summer if eating spiced food makes you
feel cooler afterwards. Unless you have some
Latin blood in your veins, the food will seem
pungent, but for eighty-five cents you can eat
a most interesting lunch consisting of an excit-
ing-looking salad soaked in a piquant sauce
and enchilladas that will make you hop, but
when you recover the gift of speech you will
admit that they are swell. And after the trial
by fire, the little crackers with cream cheese
and guava jelly will taste like nectar. And the
coffee is good.

In Grove Street (Greenwich Village) there is
Chico's, a smart Spanish night club, to which
you had better taxi. It gives you your money's
worth, however, or used to, for a two-dollar
minimum charge, and the floor show is more
attractive than most. And while we think again
of Greenwich Village, you might look around
for one of those freak but quiet little places
built to look like boats or dens or cabins or
lairs. Lunch in one on a hot day if it is summer.
Some of them open out on to gardens, tiny
plots of grass where you may hear the pleasant
rattling of a lawn mower or see a woman weed-
ing as unconcernedly as if she were in a New

England village or in Sussex. It is pleasant to
be tucked away in down town New York with
perhaps only the tinkle of a piano and an occasional distant taxi hoot to remind you that you
are not on an ocean liner or in some Cape
Cod resort.

The ten places I have mentioned are not
necessarily the ten best in New York, and some
of them may not now exist, but if you are
staying long enough in New York to want
more, you should certainly learn to acquire a
collection for yourself. The ones I have listed
are all reasonably priced, Sardi's and Chico's
being the most expensive of the ten. I have
left a multitude unmentioned, from Beef-
steak Charlie's to Child's. Names like Bre-
voort, Schraffts and Longchamps rise and
look at me reproachfully. I knew it was a
mistake to begin getting down to details.

Most of the best stores or shops in New York
are on Fifth Avenue, which rises matter of
factly and disappears humbly but which in
its middle section is Piccadilly, Bond Street,
Berkeley Street, Regent Street, Oxford Street
and the Haymarket rolled into one. However brief your stay in New York you should
walk from 59th Street (Central Park South)
down Fifth Avenue as far as 34th Street and
back on the other side, a total journey of fifty
blocks, and you can make it last five hours,

and if you like, walk at least five miles in the various stores into which you dip *en route*.

Fifth Avenue is New York. There are stores, and fascinating stores, on other avenues and on streets east and west of Fifth Avenue, but there is no getting away from the fact that anything bought on Fifth Avenue and stating as much on the label has an air about it of elegance combined with a businesslike smartness that no other avenue, except in certain instances Madison, attains. Here are Department Stores and Specialty Shops for men and women, Altman at 34th Street, Lord and Taylor's at 38th, Saks Fifth Avenue at 49th and De Pinna at 52nd.

For women there are Bests at 35th, Bergdorf Goodman at 58th, Bonwit Teller at 56th, Peck and Peck at 47th and 55th, and the little Kayser stores at 41st and 45th.

For men there are Finchley at 46th, John David at 43rd, Knox at 40th and 55th, and Dobbs at 57th.

Cartier and Tiffany are the fashionable jewellers, Gunther and Jaeckel are specialists in furs, Spaldings will supply you with anything you may need for sport, and Dunhill's and Benson and Hedges will see to your smoking needs. Abercrombie and Fitch, sporting and clothing store, was on Fifth Avenue, but has since moved across to Madison.

You can get anything you want on Fifth Avenue from a hen's egg to a suite for a world cruise.

57th Street, which has the appearance of one of the best avenues, is a good street in which to shop, whether your shopping takes the form of actually buying or just looking. There are numerous little art galleries on 57th Street, and these are worth looking at. There are also several restaurants, quiet hotels and attractive office buildings, giving it quite a Fifth Avenue flavour.

Broadway has some department stores, the most famous being Macy's at 34th Street, a tour of which at Christmas time is an adventure in itself. Gimbel's, almost as famous, is on Sixth Avenue at 33rd Street.

Wanamaker's, another of the well-known stores, is on Broadway at 8th Street, a little out of the way unless you happen to have other business down town.

On Lexington Avenue at 59th there is Bloomingdale's, and if your passion for department stores is such that these few are insufficient, you can watch the papers for advertisements of sales.

Near the Grand Central Terminal, in fact right at the side of it in the narrow street called Vanderbilt Avenue at 43rd Street, is a shop you should see. It is Charles, and you buy fruit there, among other things. On Madison Avenue is Fortnum and Mason's New York store and not far from it is a delightful shop that specializes in hooked rugs.

To drop from elegance with a heavy bump, there are Woolworth's Stores in New York, and they are so like Woolworth's Stores in London or the English provinces that you might be in either continent except that in the one they reckon in pence and in the other in cents. Moreover the department entitled "Notions" will mean nothing to you if you are in an American Woolworth's for the first time.

Over on Lexington Avenue in the upper fifties and sixties, you will find a number of antique shops and shops specializing in Jewish and Russian brasses. Here you can buy candlesticks and lanterns and door-knockers, and they are sometimes very worth while, especially if you have no time to go down town to Allen Street, which is brass town itself and where you can get the same things for half the price or, if you are a good bargainer, for a quarter of it.

By this time you should be tired of shopping, especially if it is summer and very hot, or winter, and bitterly cold, and New York can be both.

For your evening entertainment, New York offers you a choice of some forty or fifty theatres.

There are more, but as in London some are
closed for long periods at a time. There are
cinemas, euphemistically called "theatres"
and popularly called "movies," and these, as
in most cities, are far more numerous than the
legitimate theatres.

Seats in New York legitimate theatres cost
anything from one dollar and sixty-five cents
up, the usual scale being 1.65, 2.20, 2.75, 3.30,
4.40, but you can sometimes reserve seats at
one dollar and ten cents or even fifty-five
cents. There is much less standing in queues
(lines in America) than in Britain. Americans
have too much to do, and would rather pay
more and not waste the time standing, the
argument being that they could make double
the money saved by doing something during
the hour or so of waiting. Not that they would,
but they could.

As in Britain, there are agencies, reputable
and disreputable. In Times Square there is the
famous Gray's Drugstore, where you can get
cut rates on theatre tickets, but only, naturally,
on shows which are not doing very well, or
which are just about to close. However, it
occasionally happens that you want to see
one of these shows, and it is better to get your
ticket cheaply than to pay the full price for it.

Never patronize the men who try to sell you
theatre tickets on the sidewalk. They are

particularly pressing outside the Metropolitan Opera House. Ignore them firmly.

The prices at the Opera House are not as exorbitant as most British people imagine, though at two or three or four dollars apiece, they are enough, I admit. I have known British people, however, who have never attempted to see an opera in New York, because someone had told them that it was quite impossible to get in. Most of the boxes are privately owned, and for that reason are just a little more exciting to sit in.

You do not buy a programme in American theatres. You are given one. In some theatres and for some special plays, someone may try to sell you a souvenir programme before you get inside. Unless you really want these lavish documents at twenty-five cents each, refuse to buy one. The free programme system is too good to jeopardize. The lady or gentleman who tries to sell you the souvenir programme may tell you that you cannot get any other kind inside. Don't believe them. Go inside and you will generally get your programme as usual.

As in Britain, you are expected to check your hat and coat and tip the attendant when you take them out at the end of the performance, but if you are really hard up you can just ignore the pressing attentions of the man who tries to shame you into leaving them in his care. Ten cents is the usual tip, but you can leave fifteen or twenty-five if you are feeling generous. The attendants have a habit of leaving the quarters in full view and pocketing the dimes, hoping that the sight of a dozen quarters flatly spread on a ledge will shame you into putting a quarter down too instead of the dime you originally intended.

If you are in a hurry and have a train to catch, don't believe the attendant who tells you that there is no waiting afterwards for your hat and coat. They may do their best, but there is always waiting. And in the summer, when you have a hat only and are hard up, don't check it. Most theatres provide a wire arrangement underneath the seat for holding your hat. The attendant will probably lie to you about this, but it's almost always there, whatever he may say. If you are not hard up, check your hat. The summer is a tough time for cloak-room attendants.

At all events, the American theatre treats you pretty fairly. It does not, as some British theatres do, charge you for your programme, charge you sixpence, payable in advance, for your coat, and then expect a tip on top of the sixpence, which you would probably have given anyway.

The drawback about booking seats at the

American theatre is that they will never show
you the seats you are buying, and there is no
plan visible near the box office. Moreover,
many box office attendants have no hesitation
in telling you that your seats are centre when
they are smack against the side wall. After a
little experience, however, you will know your
theatres so well that you will dare, upon
occasion, to bicker with the attendant. The
attendant will usually win.

In New York, as in Paris, you must be
certain of what you are willing to spend, and
not be ashamed to admit when you have
reached your limit. If you pay more than you
can afford for anything, you are a sucker, and
anyone can fool you by just playing on your
vague sense of shame.

Refreshments are served in New York
theatres, but in afternoon performances there
is not the rush for tea that there is in an English
theatre, and therefore not the clink of teacups
going on well into the third act and distracting
the leading lady in her tensest moments. The
American middle-class dinner is eaten at six
o'clock or six-thirty, so a play ending at five just
gives a good housewife time to take the Subway
home to Brooklyn or the Bronx and open a
few cans for the evening meal.

Most of the New York theatres are clustered
around Broadway on the streets that run east

and west between the famous 42nd Street and 50th Street. In advertising, they are marked East of Broadway or West of Broadway, the bulk being West of Broadway. All the theatres of importance being between Sixth and Eighth Avenues, they are all on West streets, the most popular being 42nd Street, 45th Street and 48th Street.

You generally choose a theatre for the play that happens to be on there, but you should see inside the Metropolitan Opera House and take a glance at the Empire, both of them left a little in the cold on 40th Street, and the Guild Theatre on West 52nd Street where some of Eugene O'Neill's plays were first produced.

Down town on 14th Street near Sixth Avenue there is the Civic Repertory Theatre where Eva Le Gallienne has done more for the American Theatre than the British ever dreamed when they let her leave her native country some years ago now. Farther east there are a Yiddish Theatre, a Chinese Theatre and an Italian Theatre. There used to be an Irish Theatre somewhere down town, but I tried in vain to find it, in spite of the willing services of the Free State Travel Agency and an Irish priest. Theatres, restaurants and small stores are such uncertain places to mention. A week after you have noted them down, they may have disappeared for ever.

E—a

In American cinemas there is generally supposed to be no smoking, but the rule is often broken. The prices range from about thirty-five cents to two dollars. Newsreel theatres are usually twenty-five cents. Altogether, the prices are about the same as in England. Away from New York you will find special cheap movie theatres at which you can see the films you missed when they were new and more expensive. New York has one or two small movie theatres, not cheap, but not dear either, that show especially good movies that have long since passed out of the general showing. After trying to see "The Guardsman" all over the U.S.A. I finally caught it in the Little Carnegie Theatre on West 57th Street. The Fifth Avenue Cinema down town near 14th Street used to show foreign films of distinction, and probably still does. The daily lists in the *New York Times* and other papers will generally give you enough entertainment material to last a week. Hotels not only in New York but in other cities, can occasionally be persuaded to give you lists or booklets of local attractions. The trouble is that there are so many in New York that you are bewildered and so few in other cities that you are desperate.

If you are interested in docks and boats, you will find them on the Hudson River, or North

River, as the shipping authorities always call it, anywhere from West 11th Street down town up to West 59th Street on a level with Central Park South. There are docks in Hoboken and Brooklyn and on the East River and Staten Island, but in the strip of forty-eight blocks mentioned you can see boats of the United States Lines, Cunard-White Star Line, and large French, German and Italian boats.

While you are concentrating on the Hudson you should make sure of driving the length of Riverside Drive and of seeing the George Washington Bridge which spans the Hudson River at 178th Street. There is a smaller and older Washington Bridge that crosses the Harlem River at 181st Street, and there are some interesting bridges across the East River, but if you have time or inclination for only one bridge, make it the George Washington. It is a slender, beautiful thing, and if you cross it to Jersey side and sit on the cliffs there you can watch the bridge change from its daylight strength and firmness through an evening sky until it looks so unreal and fairylike twinkling gaily over the water that you can scarcely imagine the sweat and the millions of dollars that built it, and the swarming cars full of people that cross it every minute of the day.

If you are very lucky indeed the United States Fleet will be in the Hudson, and that is

a sight that stirs the whole town.   Times
Square is twice as crowded and the streets seem
full of sailor pants and porkpie caps and fuller
than usual of the lasses that love them.

The West Side used to be the fashionable
side of New York and the East mostly slum,
but in recent years the best people have taken
to living right on the edge of the East River,
and the fashionable Madison and Park Avenues
were always, of course, east of Fifth Avenue.
Some of the apartment houses overlooking the
East River are very sumptuous, with swimming
pools on the ground floor and terrace gardens
over the water. Some of them, especially those
with children of wealthy families living in them,
have alarm bells attached to every door, and
if these doors are opened by unauthorized per-
sons, a bell rings in the nearest police station
and continues to ring until the police arrive.

Whether you are interested in churches or
not you should see Saint Patrick's on Fifth
Avenue at 50th Street and the Cathedral of
Saint John the Divine at 111th Street and
Morningside Drive, and when you are down
town, Trinity Church at the junction of Broad-
way and Wall Street. You will want to see
Wall Street, anyway, just out of curiosity.

As for the tall buildings for which New York
is famous you can either just look at them from
below or you can climb one (by elevator,

unless there is an elevator operators' strike in progress) and look at the others from it. You can also fly over them and you can see them from boats on the rivers or in the harbour.

You may not be curious to know what they are but quite prepared to accept them in bulk or singly for observation purposes. If you are curious, look at the Empire State Building, the Chrysler Building, the Chanin Building, the Heckscher Building, the Metropolitan Life Building, the New York Central Building and the Grand Central Terminal with it, the Pennsylvania Station (not a sky-scraper), the Woolworth Building, the City Bank Building, the Irving Trust Building, the Fuller Building and such hotels as the Sherry Netherland, the Savoy Plaza and the Park Central.

Most of them are tall and some of them are beautiful. Many have observation towers and you can view the city from various angles, and if height exhilarates you, New York can give you all the exhilaration you want.

Don't imagine that New York is the only city with tall buildings. You can view Chicago, Cleveland, Detroit, Los Angeles, Minneapolis, Philadelphia and many other cities from observation towers and the views you get are not to be despised.

For those who want to know how the other half lives, even in America, there are the

Aquarium, as far down town as you can get without falling into the harbour, and Bronx Park Zoo, over the Harlem River into the next borough between East 180th Street and East 190th Streets.

There are three buildings in New York which every conscientious tourist visits. They are all worth while and you will have missed something if you miss them, but you can know New York tolerably well and yet never step inside them. Ask any New Yorker.

They are the New York Public Library on Fifth Avenue, between 40th and 42nd Streets, the Metropolitan Museum of Art on Fifth Avenue, against Central Park opposite East 82nd Street, and the American Museum of Natural History, on the other side of the Park at Central Park West and 77th Street. The Public Library contains more than books and the lions outside it are as familiar a meeting place as the clock in Charing Cross Station.

And in the Metropolitan Museum of Art you can see Cézanne's "L'Estaque," Degas's "At the Milliner's," Monet's "Sunflowers," Renoir's "By the Seashore," Dürer's "Saint Anthony" engraving, Reynolds's "Georgiana Elliott," Mantegna's "Lady of Rank," and Holbein's "Lady Guildford" among others no less lovely and famous.

New York is at its best in the spring and the

fall. The sunshine is soft on the stonework of the buildings, and although there is not the brilliance of winter and summer with a sunbeam flaring on the chromium plating of some of the sky-scraper tops, the city has a discreet and faintly withdrawn quality.

Drive into Central Park from the north and go south in the early evening, when the huge and graceful buildings are beginning to be lighted up. The whole sky is luminous and the lights are not glaring but soft, and the oddly spaced squares down the whole face of one of the buildings will have rose red, flame red, pale orange and lemon yellow glowing between the narrow strips of curtains.

It is fun just to be in New York, whatever the season and whatever you are doing, whether walking its streets, riding its traffic, dancing on its floors or eating at its tables.

At one-fifteen a.m. on my first night in New York, much too excited to sleep, I wrote a letter to England. Not that I had anything but the most commonplace things to record. After the quiet purposefulness of the boat sliding up the Hudson, past the huddled sky-scrapers of Manhattan and docking in the most matter-of-fact fashion, there was a brief dash in a taxi and then solitude on the fourteenth floor of a hotel, which solitude I could break at any moment by switching on the radio or telephoning the resident barber, broker, beauty salon, chiropodist, dentist, doctor, florist, garage, library or valet service. I had an insane desire to do all these things, one after the other, but I restrained myself and did none of them. Instead, I had a bath and went out and after an hour's walk had a meal in a cafeteria, by way of adventure.

The place was unexciting, or would have been on any other night, but my fifty cent cold salmon and salad, a glass of milk and a huge slice of apple pie seemed like nectar at the time. It was a hot, dry night, and I was not really very hungry. I now have no idea where that cafeteria was. Later, I developed a fine scorn for cafeterias, and must have often passed that same one unknowingly on my way to some more lavish eating-place, none of which could ever have quite the magic of that shining place that September night.

All I remember of the impressions of that first night is thinking that Broadway looked rather like a shabby Shaftesbury Avenue, that Fifth Avenue looked better, and that there were trees in New York, delicate, lacy ones, dark against the white of the buildings.

Just before I went to bed, I took a fearful peep (or peek) out of the window. It seemed miles and miles to the street.

Can you pronounce correctly and without hesitation, Arkansas, Tucson, Des Moines, Sault Sainte Marie, Yosemite, Wilkes Barre and Spokane?

Can you tell a Philadelphian from a Bostonian and a Bostonian from a Southerner?

Can you give the American equivalents for dustbin, lorry, biscuit, stud and goods-train?

Can you quote any funnier place-names than Goodnight, Inspiration and Climax?

If not, read Chapter II.

CHAPTER II

THERE is, according to Mr. Mencken, an American language. If you are under the impression that any English speech is better than any American speech you had better not go to America at all, since you will be mortified to find a large number of people speaking better American than you can ever hope to speak, and about half that number speaking better English than many of the people you know in England, unless you happen to move among people who speak very good English, and few of us, alas, do that.

By "better" speech, I mean clearer, firmer, livelier and more beautiful speech. There is not a great deal of difference between good English and good American. English is more clipped and clearer in its dental consonants, American is smoother, and clearer in its vowels and the liquid consonant R; English is more varied in its intonation, but American in its monotony of intonation sounds strong and firm and masculine in contrast to the effeminate qualities of some of the affected English heard in the south of England.   In vocabulary, English remains staid and conservative. American, with a rapidly changing vocabulary, loses dignity but gains in freshness and liveliness. Remember that slang and what are known as foreign impurities in language are a constant source of richness and development of vocabulary.   English ceased to be pure Anglo-Saxon before the Norman Conquest.   American began to break away from seventeenth-century English three hundred years ago.

As for beauty of speech, that is a matter of taste, but if you hear beauty in Dublin Irish, the speech of a Kentish yokel and the cultured English of His Majesty the King, you are likely to find much that is delightful to listen to in the Southern speech of the Carolinas, in the dry New England tones of Vermont, in the stage speech of New York and the very excellent speech of President Roosevelt.

You need not bother about American spelling unless you are a stickler for doing exactly as Rome does when you are in Rome.   The few hundred instances in which American spelling differs from English are rarely indicative of a change in pronunciation.   The commonest examples are "honor" for "honour" and similar words, one "l" for two in "woollen," "traveller" and other words, and simplifications like "check" for "cheque" and "jail" for "gaol." Any American can understand what you write, however, and Americans themselves argue hotly on the subject of simplified spelling in such words as "nite," "thru" and "altho."

You should be able to make yourself easily understood in America, and this is not difficult. It is no good going on the assumption that if an American in Britain speaks indistinctly and makes mistakes in pronunciation, he is gauche, but that if you speak indistinctly and make mistakes in pronunciation in America, the millions of Americans who live there are gauche and incapable of speaking their native language. No indeed. You yourself are gauche, and not only gauche, but stupid and pigheaded.

I do not suggest that you should adopt an American accent the minute you land. The average Englishman's attempt at good, or bad, American is pathetic and far far worse than the average American's imitation of Cockney or Mayfair. If you doubt this, listen to a New York company playing "The Barretts of Wimpole Street," and then hear a London company wrestling with "Street Scene."

You should, when in America, speak distinctly and without affectation, and be at least aware of some of the more vital differences in pronunciation and usage even if you have no intention of making things easier for the Americans by using them. And you should know how to pronounce the more tricky American place names.

Between forty and fifty of these are worth noting, and here they are, beginning with the names of twenty-three of the forty-eight states:

Wyoming	Stress on "o," rhyming with "homing."
Nebraska	"Ask" has the "at" quality as in Northern English and American "ask," not the Southern English "ahsk" quality, which sounds comic to an American (except a Bostonian who will make "starved" sound more like "stabbed" and yet will say "ahsk" with the best Londoner).
Louisiana *Montana* *Indiana*	Similarly, ending like the girl's name Anna, not "ahna." You can, however, use the "ah" sound in Nevada and Colorado.
Illinois	Stress on final syllable, which rhymes with "boy."
Arkansas	Final syllable pronounced "saw." Stress the first syllable and skip lightly over the second, forget-

	ting that it has any connection with Kansas.
Kansas	As you would expect, with stress on first syllable and the final "s" sounded. The first "s" is pronounced "z." The first syllable is "can." Don't attempt anything like "kahn."
Ohio	Stress on second syllable. Oh-high-o.
Iowa	Stress on first syllable. 'Igh-(owa). Whatever you do don't stress the "o" and don't put a cockney "r" at the end. If you must be very corn belt and palooka you can say "Ioway," but it sounds funny from an Englishman.
Michigan	Stress on first syllable, and the "ch" is pronounced "sh," not "tch."
Tennessee	Stress on final syllable.
Vermont	Stress on final syllable.
Oklahoma	Stress on first and third syllables. And the first syllable is "oak," not "ock."
Missouri	Stress on second syllable. Pronounce "ss" as "z." Some local people say "mizzourah" but you needn't.

Dakota   Stress on second syllable.

Idaho   Stress on first syllable, which is a
                diphthong as in the girl's name
                "Ida."   Skip lightly over the
                second syllable.

Oregon   Stress the first syllable and skip
                lightly over the second.

Connecticut   Stress on second syllable, and omit
                the second "c." Say "Connet-
                ticut" but don't hit the "t" too
                hard.

Massachusetts
Minnesota } Stress on third syllable.
Arizona

Utah   Stress on first syllable, which is
                "You."   The second syllable
                varies between "tah" and "taw."

The remaining states present no difficulties.
Some pronunciations of other place-names,
however, might be helpful.

Adirondacks   Stress on "ron." The "i" is short.

Alleghenies   Stress on third syllable. Rhymes
                with "zanies."

Chicago   "Sh" sound, never "tch."

Tucson   "Two-Son," rhyming with
                "gone." Don't sound the "c."
                And when I say "gone" I mean
                the usual British pronunciation.

Groton   "Graw-ton." Stress on first syl-
                lable.

Des Moines	"de-Moyn." Stress on second syllable.
Saint Paul	Pronounce "Saint" in full, not "s'nt."
Saint Louis	"Saint" as above. "Louis" is a bone of contention. Some people say Saint Lewis, and others say Saint Looey.
Louisville	Simple. Always "Looeyville."
Sault Sainte Marie	"Soo-Saint-Maree," Marie having the stress on the second syllable and" Sainte" having its full sound.
Concord	Stress on first syllable. The name sounds like the Southern English pronunciation of "conquered."
Wilkes Barre	The second name of the compound has two syllables, sounding more like the English "berry" than "barry."
Butte	"Bute."
Houston	"Hughes-ton," not Hooston.
Mobile	"-eel," not "-isle."
Miami	"My-ammy" or "My-ammah." Stress on second syllable which is short as in English "can."
Cincinnati	Stress on "at" which has the quality of the English "at," not of the Southern English "ask."

Toledo   Make no attempt at Spanish pro-
                    nunciation.   It is "Toleedo"
                    with the stress on the second
                    syllable.

Ottawa   Stress on first syllable.   Skip
                    lightly over the others.   Ottawa
                    shouldn't be here.   It's in
                    Canada.

Los Angeles   Stress on first syllable of the
                    second word.   And you can say
                    "angeless" with a hard "g"
                    (as in "dog") or with a "dge"
                    sound (as in "angel").   Either
                    will pass, and it is better to say
                    "less" or "liss" than "leas."
                    The final syllable is unstressed.

Omaha   Stress on first and third syllables.
                    If you are Southern English
                    and r's mean nothing to you,
                    start to say Omar Khayyám
                    and then say Omar-hah, or
                    Omar-haw.   If you sound your
                    r's, don't try this method.   Like
                    Utah, the last vowel varies with
                    different speakers.

Yosemite   Stress on "sem" and the word has
                    four syllables.   "Yo-Semitty."

New Orleans Stress "Orl" and skip over "eans"
                    quickly.   Some people say
                    "leens" with a strong stress.   As

long as you don't make three syllables of the second word, your effort will pass.

Terre Haute "Terrahote" or "Terrahut" or almost anything that isn't good Parisian. I never met a native of Terre Haute and I was never in the city.

Albuquerque Stress on third syllable, rhyming with "perky."

El Paso Take your time over this one. Use the American flat "a," that is, more like "pal" than "pa," and pronounce the "s" as "z."

Milwaukee Stress on second syllable, which is usually short—"wockie."

Detroit Stress the second syllable, and sound the final t.

Cheyenne Stress the second syllable, "Shyenn," but the American "e" being flatter than the Southern English, it is more like a Londoner's pronunciation of "Shy-Anne."

Woonsocket Stress the first and third syllables. Don't stress the "sock."

Pawtucket Stress the "tuck." Skip lightly over the "paw."

Cornwall Stress "corn," but don't leave the "wall" quite unstressed.

Ogunquit	Stress on "gun."
Duluth	Stress on second syllable "looth." The "th" is voiceless, as in "thin."
Missoula	As in Missouri, the "ss" is sounded "z." Stress on second syllable.
Schenectady	Stress on second syllable, and "sk" initially, not "sh," as in the American "sk" pronunciation of "schedule."
Spokane	Stress on second syllable, but don't skip over the first. The second syllable rhymes with "man," not with "mane."

There are variant pronunciations for some of these, but you will be safe with the ones given.

If I have made any errors, and I am confident enough to think that I have made none, I apologize, first of all to America, and secondly to whomsoever I may have misled.

I listened very carefully, however, in America, and made local enquiries in many instances, and asked to be corrected whenever I mispronounced an American place-name.

One warning. Don't place your trust in the statements of one single American, especially if he is in Europe and has little linguistic training. He has probably not travelled widely in his own country but would hardly like to admit to an Englishman his inability to pronounce correctly any place-name in it. I have heard New Englanders mispronounce western names and Southerners mispronounce New England names. You may recollect that the London pronunciation of Machynlleth and Auchtermuchty leaves much to be desired, and you cannot expect every New Yorker to feel at home with Waxahachie and Pemigewasset.

The differences in actual sounds between American and English are not so important as differences of vocabulary and syntactical usage.

The chief differences, however, taking for American a speech not excessively coloured with Southernisms or New Englandisms, and for English ordinary unaffected educated London speech, are in the "r" sound in such words as "murder" and the respective vowels in such words as "but," "fast," "dog" and "cough."

The "r" is very strong in the Middle West and swamps the whole vowel, weaker in the east and almost non-existent in the south.

In England this "r" is also non-existent in the educated south and is nothing like the trilled "r" of Wales and Scotland. In Southern Ireland the "r" almost approximates to the American, and some of the southern and midland English counties have the actual sound among rural speakers. I have heard it in uneducated Sussex, Kentish and even Lancashire speakers, and it gives the familiar "burr" to western English country speech.

The "u" in "but" is pronounced in America as a Welshman pronounces it. A Londoner pronounces it almost as a Scotsman pronounces "bat." In a word like "hurry" the American sounds more like the pronoun "her" followed by "y," the "r" being strongly sounded.

Every Englishman is familiar with the American pronunciation of words like "fast," "can't," "path," and "laugh," but most Englishmen trying to imitate Americans reproduce the same sound in "barn," "park" and "car." In most of the States, however, the vowel here is just like our own southern English, but with the "r" colouring. Only in Boston and the country parts of eastern New England do you "pairk your cair" and in the Southern states you even "pahk yo' cah." Certain people in Philadelphia "pork their cors," but it is better to leave them quite alone.

The "o" of "dog" in America is slightly flattened and was once very snappy English. When the gallants of the seventeenth century Restoration said "gad" they were not rhyming it with "bad" as spoken by a modern Londoner but with "bad" as spoken by a Scot. Americans occasionally approximate to "gad" themselves. "Gawd" is sometimes heard in America, but never "Gord."

"Cough" and "coffee" are not "cawf" and "cawffee" nor are they "cahf" and "cahffee." They are something in between these two sounds and the length and quality of the vowel varies with different speakers.

The difference in British and American intonation is much more important, and this cannot be described on paper except by a series of odd-looking curves and dashes. The only thing to do is to listen to the tune of American speech and become familiar with it.

Remember that a pure English pronunciation spoken to an American tune will pass for American nine times out of ten, but American pronunciation spoken with an English tune will simply sound false and very funny to any American.

The reverse is also true. If an educated easterner, say a citizen of Hartford, Connecticut, came to England and used exactly the same sounds that pass for good American in Hartford but spoke them to the English intonation, not one Englishman in twenty would know him as an American.

The reason is this. Almost every sound used in American dialects is used somewhere in some British dialect. No British dialect contains the same collection of sounds as any one American dialect, but almost every American pronunciation of simple words can be paralleled or nearly paralleled in some part of Britain.

The intonation, or tune, however, is entirely foreign and nothing like the English, the Welsh, or the Scottish speech tunes. Irish is the nearest to American in tune, but even there it does not take a sensitive ear to distinguish the differences.

So much for intonation.

Many English people imagine that all Americans use slang. On the contrary, many of them use no slang at all, though new expressions are not looked upon with so much disfavour and suspicion as in Britain.

It is better for British people to avoid slang. It sits badly on British speech and sounds as inappropriate as a Chicago banker looks in a Venetian gondola. Moreover, the English are known all over America for the slowness of their humour and for their well-meaning use of out-of-date American slang. Slang changes very quickly and what is correct (in slang) in 1935 will be passé and dumb English in 1940.

Some innocent English expressions can be singularly unfortunate if used in America. Avoid the term "knocked up," referring to the person who raps on your door in the morning. In American slang it means "pregnant."

And you can save yourself a great deal of bewilderment and the American you meet much embarrassment if you refrain from using any English phrase with the words "peckish" and "pecker" in it. There are other unfortunate remarks you can make, but I do not propose to cover the whole field of obscene terminology, and a gentle warning should be sufficient.

If you are in the habit of using the word "bloody" in English, you will find that its meaning is literal and quite innocent in America. Therefore, waste no venom on it, whatever the provocation. You will soon learn its American equivalents.

I now give a list of the more important differences of usage in vocabulary.

ENGLISH	AMERICAN
luggage	baggage
dustbin	ashcan
jug	pitcher
sea	ocean
railway	railroad
bonnet (of a car)	hood
hood (of a car)	top
tramcar	trolley car, street car or surface car
tinned	canned
blinds (window)	shades

ENGLISH	AMERICAN
glass (of a watch)	crystal
promenade	boardwalk
sweets	candy
cutting (newspaper)	clipping
bowler (hat)	derby (not pronounced darby)
lift (the noun)	elevator
goods train	freight train
ironmonger's	hardware store
angry	mad
braces	suspenders
suspenders	garters
films, pictures	movies
stalls (in a theatre)	orchestra
booking office(station)	ticket office
post free	post paid
assistant (in a shop)	salesgirl, saleswoman, salesman
commercial traveller	traveling salesman (one "l")
bookshop	bookstore
bootlace, shoelace	shoestring
tap	faucet
mineral waters	soft drinks, sodas, pops
ill	sick
lorry	truck
board school, free school, council school	public school
public school (as Eton)	prep school (as Andover)

ENGLISH	AMERICAN
sweet	dessert (whether fruit or not)
porridge	oatmeal
any patent breakfast food	cereal
return (ticket)	round trip
single (ticket)	one way
Ltd. (limited)	Inc. (incorporated)
shell fish	sea food
rise (advance in salary)	raise
underdone (meat)	rare
post (verb and noun)	mail
postman	mail carrier, letter carrier
petrol	gasoline, gas
petrol station	filling station, gas station
flat	apartment
insects(including moths, flies, etc.)	bugs
public lavatory	toilet, rest room, comfort station, washroom
form (telegraph or income tax)	blank
label (gramophone records)	seal
pack (of cards)	deck
puff puff (infant speech for train)	choo choo

ENGLISH	AMERICAN
gee up (to a horse)	giddy up
biscuit	cracker, cookie
scone	biscuit
puncture (tyre)	flat, flat tire ("i")
mending punctures	fixing flats
peep (verb)	peek, take a peek
trousers	pants
tie	necktie
stud	collar button
autumn	fall
funnel	smokestack
dickie seat	rumble seat
pavement	sidewalk
concrete (of road surface)	pavement
slippery (of road surface)	slick
ices	ice cream

There are some words used in America with the same meanings as in Britain but with quite a different pronunciation. Here are some of the most important:

ENGLISH	AMERICAN
laboratory	Five syllables. Stress on first and fourth, "lab" and "or."
detail	Stress on second syllable
schedule	"sk" sound
figure	"figyure," not "figger."

ENGLISH	AMERICAN
ate	Rhymes with "pate." "Et" is ignorant and rustic.
news, suit, produce (verb)	"nooze," etc. more common.
tomato	Rhymes with potato, but many Americans say "to-mahto."
lieutenant	Not "left" but "loo-tenant."
fertile, virile, futile	"Fertle," like myrtle, not "fertyle."
clerk, Berkeley, Derby	"er" as in "mercy," not "ar."
been	"bin."
trait	Final "t" sounded.
romance	Stress on first syllable.
advertisement	Stress on third syllable. Say the verb "advertize," and add "ment."
garage	Stress on second syllable. Rhymes with "mirage."
aluminium	Aluminum (Stress on second syllable) "loom."

Some Americans, anxious to speak British English, overstrain their broad "a" and say "mahss" and "fahncy", but on the whole the mid-Atlantic speech of fashionable New England is pleasant and harmless, though it lacks the richness of more natural speech.

As for syntactical differences, I shall be writing a textbook if I do any more than mention a few of them and leave the rest to your observation if you are at all interested in the American language, and if you have read as far as this, you must be.

The use of "guess" and the fact that it has a respectable pedigree in mediæval English are well known. It may not be so well known that some speakers of English who have never been to America nor come under any American influences use the word in the American sense quite naturally. English writers attempting American tend to use the word too often and sometimes use it in the wrong place. It means "think" in such a phrase as "I guess I'll go to bed" and "suppose" in the phrase "I guess that's why." But English phrases like "I think you are very beautiful" or "I suppose you wouldn't like lunch now, would you?" the American "guess" will not fit. Just as American expressions sound odd spoken with an English intonation, so an American word is frequently out of place in an English locution.

The American "sure" is either of Irish origin or, together with Irish, of English seventeenth-century origin. It is used in the Welsh language, "ie siwr," being closer to "yeah, sure" than to "yes, of course." I once heard an Englishman attempt "yeah, sure," but what he said was "yeh shaw" and the American who heard him looked puzzled.

The use of "so" in the expression "you do, so" or "good-night, so" is of Irish origin. "You do, too" is more common.

" 'Tis not.—'Tis too" is a common argument heard in America.

The Irish "yous" is heard among vulgar speakers, especially in the east, for example, "all of yous" or "yous guys." In the south, "you-all" is often used for the plural of "you," and no educated Southerner uses the expression in the singular.

"How you-all this mo'nin'?" is a southern greeting, but only to more than one person, in spite of what the Northerners say.

"Different than" is a useful locution. An Englishman's clumsy sentence, "Somehow he looked different from the way he looked the last time I saw him," becomes in American "Somehow he looked different than the last time I saw him."

"Go see," "go look" are American for "go and see," "go and look," but their simplicity is countered by the cumbersome "in back of" for the preposition "behind," though it is no more clumsy than "in front of" for the simpler, literary "before."

Referring to time, "a quarter to" and "a quarter past" are "a quarter of" and "a quarter after" in American, though in some places "fifteen minutes" is substituted for "quarter" just as the English "three-quarters" is often "three fourths" in America. The English "five-and-twenty past" is strange to an American, who says "twenty-five after." Recently, some Americans have picked up "to" and "past" and use them regularly.

If you are directing a stranger in New York, you speak in terms of blocks and corners, not of turnings, and you refer to the points of the compass more frequently, since Americans have an acuter sense of direction than most English people. It is true that the District Railway and the City and South London Railway refer to Westbound and Eastbound, North-bound and Southbound trains, but in London streets few Englishman think of the south-west corner of Oxford Circus or walking eastwards along the Strand.

"That won't hurt you any," using "any" for the English "at all" is strongly American to British ears. So are the uses of "hit" and "fix."

The old Icelandic "hitta" meant, among other things, "to meet, to come to" without any sense of violence, and in this sense the American street direction once given me in Philadelphia, "Go right ahead until you hit the cemetery wall", was not a flippant invitation to suicide.

"Fix" is generally used. You fix your hair, you fix a flat, you fix the ham and eggs, you fix people. In fact, anything or anyone you "see to" in English, you fix in American.

Pennsylvania Dutch is responsible for the quaint expression "I want out" or "Somebody wants in," with the omission of the verb, but these phrases are not general American, though they may be heard well outside Pennsylvania. They are the kind of phrase which sophisticated New Yorkers would use for comedy effect, just as they have used "pernt" and "erster" with a friendly dig at their own East Side.

A little phrase that puzzles many Europeans is "I should worry," of Yiddish origin, which neither means what it says nor precisely, "I should not worry." You can get its meaning and its intonation if you say mentally, "There is no reason why" and then, loudly and confidently, "I should worry." But don't let any American hear you whispering hastily beforehand, or the illusion will be lost.

Many words and phrases which the English regard as typical American are provincial and ignorant and never used by educated people. Some of them doubtless owe their notoriety in England through the agency of unoriginal American dramatists of the nineteenth century who introduced rustic New England characters

G—a

into their melodramas by way of comedy relief and made them say "I guess and calculate" like any stage "rube," just as England had the stage Irishman and still has the stage American, and America the stage Englishman complete with eyeglass and constant use of "by Jove" and "bally."

Provincial expressions in America creep higher, socially, in America than in England. I have heard lecturers and graduates of the best schools and colleges using the terms "somewheres," "anywheres," "anyways," "a long ways off" and even "snuck" for "sneaked" and "brung" for "brought." The majority avoid such words, but some professional people are not ashamed of them.

There is a tendency to use "some place" and "no place" for "somewhere" and "nowhere."

"Gotten" is still used, but "got" is quite as common.

English is easily understood in all parts of America provided only that the speech be slow and clear and that some regard for American differences in usage be shown. Travelled Americans are accustomed to English and many of them speak it almost faultlessly, but if you are driving in country places you must expect to be asked to repeat your remarks unless you have been generous enough to

adapt your speech and make it generally
understandable and easy to follow.

American personal names and place-names
are, I suppose, as much a part of the people as
of the language, but since the people I associated with in America were mostly concerned
with the names their parents had given them
and not with giving names to their progeny,
and no one seemed to be naming villages
when I happened to be around, we can classify
names as a linguistic institution rather than a
public habit.

The Americans have their simple, beautiful
names and their pretentious names as well.
They also have their popular middle-class
names, of which the commonest are Helen,
Ruth, Jean, Miriam, Betty, Hope, Rita and
Marie. And for men, Raymond, Gordon and
Theodore. Marie is pronounced with the stress
on the second syllable.

Some Americans have followed an old country custom of giving double names to their
daughters and always using those double names
in full. It is odd to see the most sophisticated
young ladies bearing such names as Mary
Jane, Mary Louise, Mary Elizabeth, Sarah
Jane, Sarah Emily, Emily Ann, Elizabeth
Ann, Mary Ann, Sarah Louise and Martha
Jane. Names are very much a matter of personal taste, but to me, these cottage compounds
are very delightful.

Foreign influence has broadened the range of given names, and there is a tendency on the part of the parents who in Britain would call their daughters Joan, Dorothy and Phyllis to run in America to Irma, Hermine, Sonia, Norma and Caretta for their daughters and to Otto, Carl, Leon, Adolph and Louis for their sons.

Men often have unwieldy names, and among them are Wilbur, Hamilton, Yardley, Emerson, Wesley, Luther, Barrett, Franklin, Ellsworth, Warren, Seymour, Hale, Sterling, Willis, Carroll, Sherman, Daggett, Carlton, Homer, Earl, Deane, Everett, Hudson, Irving, Milton and almost anything else you can think of. Perhaps I should not call these names unwieldy, but many Americans apparently find them so, for abbreviations are distressingly common, and within a couple of hours of knowing the "bunch" above you will be calling them Ham. or Wes. or Lute. or Em. or Dag. or Hud., just as among your friends with more ordinary names there will be Bill and Jim and Dick and Harry and Bob. And, I fear, even Art and Ed and Lou.

And among the girls, Betty, Kitty, Dot, Bee (for Beatrice), and Mim (for Miriam). Only Helen seems generally to remain unmolested (the name, that is). Even Nell and Nellie are rare.

In addition to all this abbreviation there are some nicknames, the commonest being Chuck for Charles, Red for the English Ginger, and Bud, denoting a vague friendliness and presumably cognate with the noun "buddy" and the Irish "butty."

As for surnames in America, you have only to look at lists of schools and colleges or city orchestras or social columns in newspapers to see that the foreign element is much stronger than in England. The names naturally vary with the section of the country. In New York City you will find many Jewish names, in parts of New Jersey, Hungarian names; in the mill country of north-eastern Connecticut there will be French names (from Canada); in Pennsylvania, German, Polish and Welsh names; in Boston, Irish names; in New Haven, Italian names; in Minneapolis, Scandinavian names; in Santa Fé, Spanish names and so on. Pick up a telephone book in America, the slim country ones, not the fat city ones, and the mixture will sort itself out before your eyes. It is the same with place names. In one spot in Minnesota and in another spot in Virginia there is a little clump of Welsh names. All over the country you can find in the general muddle little clumps that hark back wistfully to Ireland or Scotland or Germany or Scandinavia.

America has some of the strangest and most

beautiful names, some of the ugliest and most commonplace names in the world.

Some of the most attractive are Indian names. Manhattan is one of them, and the New England states are full of Indian names. Five New England rivers are called Connecticut, Housatonic, Quinnipiac, Merrimack and Pemigewasset. Among lakes there are Sunapee, Saranac, Winnepesaukee and Mooselookmeguntic. And Passamaquoddy Bay.

And not to be overlooked for fantastic comedy are Weogufka, Enumclaw, Wachapreague, Quonochontaug, Beowawe, Waxahachie, Wequetonsing, Choccolocco and Hatchechubbee.

You feel that Tin-pan Alley has missed a trick when it does nothing, or has done nothing up to now, with Choccolocco and Hatchechubbee.

Most of these Indian names are names describing local features, though some of them may for all I know be names of native chiefs. I should like to think that Hatchechubbee was originally the name of a vivacious squaw.

English and other settlers gave similar names, some very beautiful, using terms no longer in current use in England such as "run," "branch" and "creek." These are used in different parts of the country, according to whichever words are used. "Creek" is pronounced "crick" and always means a stream, not as in English, a cove.

Some of these local names tend to be suitable for suburban bungalows, but others are euphonious, appropriate and imaginative.

New England had a habit of taking names right off the English map, but Deep River, Swiftwater, Breadloaf, Dead River, Blue Hill, Sleeping Giant and Oak Bluffs are original and refreshing enough.

Out west and down south there are Merry Oaks, Pinetops, Cedar Bluff, Vinegar Bend, Yellow Pine, Little Creek, Honey Creek, Deep Run, Indian Run, Falls of Rough, Manyberries, Rolling Prairie, Crab Orchard, Running Water, Troutrun, Sweet Valley, Slippery Rock, Early Branch, Cherry Valley and Red Bluff.

It was simpler, however, for those settlers with more sentimentality than imagination to borrow names from European towns and villages and spread them haphazard over the American map. New England abounds in English names like Essex, Plymouth, Portsmouth, Devon, Northampton, Truro, Southampton, Bristol, Stamford, Hartford, Boston and London, and these names are to be found farther south and farther west.

One remarkable example of an eastern settlement spreading west and south and reduplicating its name as settlers moved on is Springfield.

There are one or two villages in Britain called Springfield, and the American name may either have been derived from one of these, or be a man's name, or be a purely invented one. At all events, Springfield proved to be a popular name in the States.

It began in New England, of course, and there is a Springfield in Massachusetts, quite a large one, and three smaller ones, one in Maine, one in New Hampshire and one in Vermont.

Just south of New England, there is a Springfield, New Jersey, and just west there is one in New York State. There are two in Canada, one east in New Brunswick and one farther west in Ontario.

Going to the Middle West, there are Springfields in Ohio, West Virginia, Illinois, Wisconsin, Minnesota, South Dakota and Nebraska.

Nor is the South to be outdone. There are seven southern Springfields, one each in Kentucky, Tennessee, Missouri, Arkansas, Georgia, South Carolina and Louisiana.

And in the Far West Idaho and Oregon have a Springfield apiece. The only large area to escape the Springfields would appear to be the South West.

Some humble little towns in England have become great cities in America, and in many instances the reverse has happened.

Boston on the Wash, stump and all, is insignificant compared with the great city on the Massachusetts coast, but the Manchesters and Portsmouths of America are still far behind their English parents.

English names are to be found in large quantities in the forty-eight states of the Union, and all over Canada, but traces of French occupation remain in Eastern Canada, Louisiana and various north-western and midwestern trading posts. Some great towns in the vast central plain that was once French territory still have French names. Des Moines, Terre Haute, Saint Louis and New Orleans are examples.

The Canadian French name Montreal is famous, but the host of names around them are not so well known, Beaupré, Isle aux Grues, Sainte Modeste, Sainte Louise and Lac aux Sables, to mention only a few.

And in the lower Mississippi valley, Parcperdue, Pointe a la Hache, Plaquemine, St. Bernard, St. Gabriel and St. Tammany lend a pleasant flavour to the names of Louisiana.

In California, Arizona, New Mexico and Texas there are Spanish names in hundreds. An entirely different flavour obtains where you drive through places with names like Alcalde, Santa Barbara, Montecito, Anton Chico, Las Cruces, Tajique, San Miguel, Pinos Altos, San Antonio, and, to mention the best known, Santa Fé, San Francisco and Los Angeles.

It would be a simple matter if we could stop there, but when in one section of a mid-western state we find Sveadahl, Morgan, Cambria, Le Sueur, Heidelberg, New Prague, Belle Plaine, St. Patrick, Kilkenny, Shakopee and Warsaw, with Newmarket and Lonsdale not far away, and when even in conservative New England, similar mixtures may be discovered, we have to admit that anything more than a rough classification is beyond us.

And to add to the confusion, there are the names of founders, generals and national heroes, either alone or with -town or -ville or -burg attached, and not only the names of well-known people, but also names of local men of whom nothing has since been heard. Lincoln, Washington, Lafayette and Columbus we can follow, but Smithton, Raubsville, Rebersburg and Collins mean nothing to anyone but citizens of those places and probably not much to them.

Some of the Biblical names are attractive, and are not only confined to New England. They are especially common in that section, though, in the South, and in the Quaker state of Pennsylvania, as you would expect, they fit rather pleasantly into quiet countryside regions.

Gilead, Boaz, Bethesda, Gamaliel, Zion, Sharon, Canaan, New Jerusalem, Bethlehem, Jordan, Salem, Rehoboth, Goshen and Lebanon.

Some names indicate local industries, Oil City, Zinc, Grit, Galena, Soda, Sodaville, Glo (Welsh for "coal"), Quarry, Carbondale, Gypsum, Asbestos, Petroleum Center, and a whole collection of names associated with fruit and fruit growing, of which Fruitland is the most popular, Fruitdale and Fruitvale following, with occasional competitors in the form of Fruithurst, Fruita, Fruitport and Fruit Valley.

Most of the above names command a certain admiration for their directness. There is, you feel, no nonsense about a place called Zinc or Soda, though you cannot be too sure of the Fruitlands. Personally, I rather like nonsense, but not in Fruita.

An opposite tendency is observed in names which suggest a mentality on a par with that of suburban couples in England who call their houses Cosy Nook and Bide-a-Wee and Home Sweet Home, or fashion a clumsy hybrid from the bride's and bridegroom's names.

There are many of these coy, pretentious names in America. Small villages living near state lines will blossom forth with names like Texarkana, Texhoma, Texline, Calexico, Delmar and Marydel.

The rest I can only lump in one long catalogue and leave them without comment. Some are genuine, but odd, and most of them are just stupid.

Good-night, Rosebud, Deposit, Acme, Temperanceville, Reliance, Vermilion, Puritan, Panic, Pansy, Mustard, Republic, Eureka, Searchlight, Detour, Hurry, Principio Furnace, Inspiration, Amity, Birdsong, Daisy, Jenny Lind, Magazine, Success, Climax, Sweet Home, Isle of Hope, Swink, Frostproof (Florida, of course), Oblong, French Lick, Surprise, Cylinder, Gem, Whatcheer (Iowa), Centralia, Industry, Mechanicsville, Cyclone, Gravity, Peoples, Picayune, Two Dot, Ohiowa (in Nebraska), Friendly, Frugality, Social Circle (Georgia), Gertrude, Ovid, Reform, Dixiana, Eclectic, Enterprise, Equality, Suspension, America (Alabama), Young America and Correctionville.

It all seems like one huge joke. However, I have no doubt that Britain could produce some very embarrassing specimens.

Picayune (Mississippi) is interesting. It is the name of a newspaper in New Orleans, and is an adjective in common use throughout America meaning something small and trivial. It formerly was a noun and the name of a small coin. Presumably the newspaper cost that amount and the word spread from the south all over the country in its sense of smallness and insignificance.

The tendency in the States to have names of two words is marked. Most of the natural local names quoted are of this type, and the habit of following names with City and Center, and preceding names with New or Fort helps to make names on the pattern of Carson City, Union Center, Fort Collins, and New London very common all over America.

Altogether, considering that the American place-names, with the exception of the genuine Indian ones, were mostly collected within three centuries, their quality and variety are of a high standard. I have given undue attention to freak names because they amuse me. They are mostly in very remote districts, and as far as I remember I was in only two of the fifty-eight I have listed, and I drove right through them.

How much more do you have to pay in an American train for a Pullman seat, for an Upper Berth, a Lower, a Section?

What is the "Twentieth Century Limited"?

What are small town hotels like?

Which is the "Sunshine State"?

If you would rather not know, omit Chapter III.

CHAPTER III

DRIVING AND TRAVEL

In America you can walk, hitch hike, drive a car, ride a horse or burro, take a bus or train or plane to get from one place to another. You can doubtless think of other ways of moving around, but four of the above ways are the easiest. Driving your own car or someone else's car is the best, being driven in a car is next best, the bus is cheap but painful for long distances, the train is convenient but for the most part unexciting and the plane is certainly exciting but for ordinary every-day purposes expensive, though as compared with railroad fares, plane fares are very reasonable, especially if you carry very little baggage.

Buses run almost everywhere and you can actually go by bus from New York to California, three thousand miles. Buses are best, however, for journeys of not more than a hundred and fifty miles, especially for journeys where the trains are slow and changes have to be made.

American railroads are not as expensive as

they were. Of recent years cheap trips and various privileges have been introduced, though facilities of this kind are not as numerous or generous as on British railways.

The equivalent of the third-class carriage is the day coach, where you sit, two by two each side of the aisle all the way down the length of the coach. Small compartments, as we know them, are not used. The coach costs three cents a mile, and when you consider that you can, if you wish, stay in a coach for three thousand miles, you can see that it mounts up. A Pullman car, with swivel armchairs, will cost you about a dollar a seat extra for a hundred mile trip and three dollars extra for five hundred miles.

Naturally, sleeping cars are used a great deal in America. A lower berth is usually quite adequate and you can look out of the window. Dressing and undressing demand a certain sinuousness especially if you are six feet long and weigh two hundred pounds. Your five hundred mile journey will cost you about four dollars for the night's rest, and you can usually stay in your bed until 8.0 or 8.30 if the train happens to arrive at your destination during the wee hours, and of course later if your train is just going on and on to Florida or California.

An upper berth is not as pleasant as a lower,

but costs three dollars instead of four for five
hundred miles. You climb into bed instead of
slipping into it, and you have no window. For
five dollars for the same journey, the negro
porter will give you a whole section, that is,
he will push up the roof of your lower berth
and give your six feet a little more turning
room. Of course, if this happens no one will
be sleeping above you, or one would suffocate.
But if you do not want to pay for a section and
there is no one else in the entire train, down
will come the roof over your head. It is the
railroad company's way of showing you how
vain it is to expect anything for nothing in these
days. The minimum cost of a night's rest is
about two dollars and a half, and you cannot
expect a sleeping berth on a journey of less
than 140 miles.

The day coaches on the American trains are
sometimes a little gritty and usually very hot.
A British fresh air fiend will be gasping very
quickly, but around him will be Americans
accustomed to centrally-heated houses, and
they will look very comfortable, so he will just
have to endure it.

Travelling long distances is an easy business
in America. The trains between the west and
east are full of students in June and September,
westerners or mid-westerners whose parents
have sent them to Smith and Wellesley and

Bryn Mawr and Vassar, and Yale and Harvard and Princeton, for many a college list in the eastern states will show half as many westerners and mid-westerners as easterners.

Chicago is 960 miles from New York, and the "Twentieth Century Limited" does the journey in less than seventeen hours, calling at ten or eleven stations *en route*. To travel the same distance in Britain you would have to go from John o'Groats at the northern tip of Scotland to London and then from London to Truro in Cornwall, and the total would be about 960 miles. An unhurried journey from New York to Chicago takes some twenty-one hours.

You allow twenty-two or twenty-three hours to Saint Louis, Missouri, and about thirty-two to Miami, Florida. The last nine hours of this journey are spent in Florida alone, between Jacksonville and Miami. Americans have a different sense of distance from the British.

The "Twentieth Century Limited" advertises a club car with a Barber, a Bath, a Secretary, a Dictaphone, a Valet, Stock Reports, Sporting Events, Magazines, Newspapers and Stationery, and an observation car with a maid, a telephone at terminals, lounge, more magazines, more newspapers and more stationery.

By "Sporting Events" it does not mean that you run races down the length of the entire train, but that you get the news of sporting events hot.

For all this special service you pay ten dollars. The fare itself is something over thirty dollars and for another thirty you can have a private drawing room, making a total of about seventy dollars without meals.

For less than that you can cross the entire continent in a bus with enough extra for your meals. Whether you will sleep or not is another question.

You can fly from New York to Chicago in less than six hours.

You can drive it comfortably in two days in a fast car stopping in Ohio on the way, and moderately in three days, stopping in Pennsylvania and Western Ohio. That is for the unhurried Englishman.

Remember that you are in a country where you can drive the distance from Calais to Constantinople or from Malaga to Moscow and be understood when you ask for a hamburger sandwich or pie *à la mode*, unless you happen to run into a recently immigrated Swede. You will fill up your tank at gas stations where the attendant will invariably say "You're a long ways from home" and make it sound original. You will stay in fireproof hotels called Roosevelt or Lincoln or Washington or Robert E. Lee, and unless you are observant of changes in vegetation, geological features, climate or dialect, your only sense of being "a long ways from home" will be your delight when you meet a car bearing the same coloured license plate as your own. License plates, or markers as they are sometimes called, are of different colours for the different states, and the colours change from year to year, generally alternating.

Some of the states have little emblems on their license plates, usually placed between the two sets of figures. Texas has its lone star and Louisiana its pelican. Massachusetts once had a cod, but they became sensitive about it and had it removed. There is a little poem poking fun at Boston and mentioning the cod, and perhaps similar jibes irritated them. The poem goes like this:

> The beautiful city of Boston,
> The home of the bean and the cod,
> Where the Lowells speak only to Cabots
> And the Cabots speak only to God.

Or something like that.

New Mexico in 1932 had "The Sunshine State" inscribed on the license plate. In 1933 it contented itself with a yellow plate adorned with a glaring sun with beams like the spokes of a bicycle wheel.

Some of the colour combinations are rather

attractive. The most successful are green on white, white on green, yellow on white, red on white, white on red, white on blue and blue on white. The prettiest, however, are not always the most distinct, and there is a lot to be said for black and white, and yellow and black, both very clear when clean. Occasionally a state bursts into gold or silver or the nearest thing to gold and silver that can be reproduced on a license plate.

Most car owners take the trouble to keep their plates clean and distinct and two cars of the same state will wave or shout or toot their horns when passing or overtaking in a far away state. After driving over sandy roads or in the desert or through mud, a license plate becomes so obscured as to be quite unreadable, even at a few yards distance.

The driving is usually excellent in the eastern states, in California and around Chicago and other mid-western cities. It lapses somewhat in the Middle West rural sections and is noticeably poor in Oregon and Washington if you drive north from California. Driving is especially good in New York City and Los Angeles, and brakes must be good, since a progression down a busy street is just a rush from stoplight to stoplight.

In most states you take a driving test before you are allowed a license. You answer a few questions and drive around half a dozen blocks.

The best way to see the country is to know an American with a car and to go shares on the running expenses. Many Americans enjoy seeing their own country and will be glad to be relieved at the wheel, but you must be a good driver. Americans have a very high standard of driving.

Cars are cheap in America, cheap to buy and not very expensive to hire. If three or four people share a car, travel becomes very reasonable in price. You can buy used cars in varying stages of decomposition from three hundred dollars down to twenty-five. There is, naturally, more risk of breakdown attached to the cheaper cars, but I have known of cars that cost between fifty and a hundred dollars giving no trouble at all for months and even years. If three people buy a sixty-dollar car and sell it at the end of their trip for as little as twelve dollars, they will have spent only a little over three pounds each on the actual car. Running expenses, together with insurance and the small tax and license cost, will come to far less than their total mileage priced at the railroad charges. And they will have a great deal more fun. I say three people because a normal car will accommodate three people and their baggage comfortably, if they travel lightly. Four is a little crowded if the car is small, but it can be done. I did it for nine hundred miles. Suitcases can be expressed very reasonably by train and only essentials taken in the car.

Don't ignore lights when you are driving. And find out the local rules for turning right or left at red lights. America is a large country and different rules obtain in different places. In New York you may turn right at red lights. If you want to go straight ahead you wait until the light goes green, and you don't wait on the extreme right of the road, because there may be someone behind who wants to use the privilege of turning right, and you can expect him to let you know that he is displeased if you prevent him. In many cities you must not turn right at red lights, but wait patiently until the green light appears.

In most cities you stop at the block marked by a red light even if you see it a hundred yards ahead. In New York if you see a red light anywhere ahead, you stop at the end of the block you happen to be in when the lights go red, even if your particular block has no light at all. On the avenues you can see red lights in rows five and six hundred yards ahead of you and it is important to stop promptly and not saunter along until you come to the light itself.

On entering a strange city keep your wits about you and notice what other cars are doing. Also look on the ground ahead of you for white lines and arrows indicating which way you should go at traffic intersections.

Notice also where each city chooses to hang its stoplights or in some cases merely stop signs. Some hang them boldly in the centre, and you can't very well miss seeing them, but the ones at the side may be low or may be high. Some cities will have a post standing up in the centre of the road with a small light inside and the words STOP and GO. Others will have what is called a traffic circle around which you go in an anti-clockwise direction unless the signs indicate otherwise.

Some cities have no stoplights at all, but have boulevards along which you can rip to your heart's content. But on the roads that cross the boulevards there are little bumps in the centre to warn you not to rip.

You had better obey the speed signals placed frequently on the sides of the road. It is embarrassing to be pursued by a cop. It happened to me in California, but the cop was soft-hearted and let us go free, even though we were exceeding the limit by seventeen miles an hour in a ten year old car and must have looked like hell let loose. Take particular notice of signs that read "Underpass," "Road

slick in wet weather" and "R. R. Tracks."
An underpass means that the road goes under
a bridge and it generally means also that the
road gives a nasty little twist and becomes
narrow at the bridge. To continue towards
such a place at a high speed usually means
instant death or badly burnt brakes and
scarred tyres. You can take your choice.

"Road slick in wet weather" means just
what it says, slick meaning slippery, and you
had better believe that one, too, especially if
your tyres are worn and on your sixty-dollar
car they are pretty sure to be. I speak feelingly,
because I was hurled into a ditch among the
uttermost wildernesses of Texas for the simple
reason that the road was "slick." And finding
yourself in a ditch together with an utterly
ruined car is more embarrassing even than
being pursued by a cop.

America teems with level crossings without
gates and you can meet your Waterloo at any
of them with ease. Some of them have red
lights as warnings and the trains are in the
habit of tooting or tolling a bell when they
propose to cross a public highway. The road
each side of the railroad track is often scrawled
with a large "R.R." in white paint and there are
always white posts with crossbars (rather like
crossbones) at the top, also on each side of
the tracks. And yet, cars are constantly collid-

ing with trains at these level crossings, and the car invariably suffers more than the train.

Other warnings not to be ignored are "Narrow Bridge," "End of Pavement," "Bump" and "Washboard." Where the road narrows can be a danger spot for two cars meeting, each going at the same speed and each about the same distance from the narrow place. "End of Pavement" does not mean that there is no more sidewalk. If you are observant you will have noticed that there was no sidewalk all along. Pavement means concrete surface and the end of it means a bump and a bad road. "Bump" just means bump. "Washboard," sometimes called "corduroy" means a road surface that is ribbed. There is a special technique associated with driving over washboard surfaces, but it is to be hoped that you will not meet sufficient examples to make it necessary to acquire the technique. The easterner, to whom such a surface is almost unknown, generally rattles slowly over it and hopes that the agony will be short. At a certain speed you will skim the ridges, but a light car will also skid at the same speed, and you should recollect that American cars, being high-powered and lightly made, tend to skid much more easily than English cars.

Altogether you will see an interesting variety of notices for your perusal on the sides of the highways, a few of them helpful but most of them advertisements of the cheapest and most imbecile kind. Some of them are planted in series so that you read a word or two at a time, but believe me, they are not generally worth the attention of intelligent people. I might warn you that "Chicken Dinner—5 cents" does not mean precisely what it says. Of course, no one but a half-wit would suppose that it did, but not even Plato could guess that it refers to candy.

If you are out of your car and just walking, don't forget that traffic runs on the right of the road in America. Everyone knows that, but you'd be surprised how many people forget, even Americans who have never been out of the country. The hospitals are always full.

Don't jay walk. That is, don't cross a road except at the proper crossing places, which are always at the end of the block.

Don't cross roads against a red light. In some cities, the police officer will call you back for this.

A few words on hitch hiking.

It is the custom in America for people of all kinds to indicate to drivers of cars on roads that they would like a lift. Outside some of the large cities where the main highways join, dozens may be seen waiting and hoping that a driver with room in his car will stop and pick one up. Fortunately, they usually wait in ones or twos along the road, so if you decide to stop, you will not have to choose among several. Some of the waiting people are travelling salesmen with little attache cases, some are college boys wanting to go from town to town without paying the railroad fare, in fact, without paying any fare, some are elderly women, some young women, though young women usually for their own safety wait in pairs and will not accept rides singly. Some are labourers, field and town, and some are coloured. Some want to go only a mile or two along the road, others will stay with you all day. Some have destinations a thousand miles away and you are just one out of twenty or thirty cars that help them on their way.

You are warned not to stop and admit strangers into your car, especially if you are alone and driving in lonely and unfamiliar country. If you are timid and careful you will miss a great deal of fun and many interesting talks with all kinds of people. You may, of course, be held up or shot or knifed or seduced, but those things can really happen anywhere and if you use some discrimination when you choose the people you pick up, you will doubtless play the good Samaritan to scores of people and never have any trouble at all.

Occasionally, if you are driving a long distance, you will prefer not to have to talk to anyone or have anyone by you. So long as you can keep an even balance and only be generous when you want, you will solve for yourself the problem of hitch hikers. If you never pick up a stranger, even when you would really like a little company, you are denying yourself and others, and if you stop too frequently or choose your riders indiscriminately or feel guilty every time you pass a pointing thumb, you are making yourself unnecessarily uncomfortable and losing the pleasure of your trip.

The best way to see things from the hitch hiker's point of view is to find yourself stranded for some reason in a lonely part of the country and have to walk many miles to the nearest garage. Unless you are very proud indeed, you will think your plight a legitimate excuse for waving an arm or jerking a thumb at likely looking cars so that you can go back the more quickly to your own. Once you have started walking you will not be associated with your stationary car and treated as a person in trouble but you will be judged on the merits of your appearance or according to the principles of the driver of the car that passes you. It is humiliating to see how many cars, with plenty of room inside them, pass you by and offer you no assistance, and when a car finally stops thirty yards ahead of you your first thought is not amazement that the fool driver is risking robbery or murder or something worse than death, but, as you climb in, gratitude and relief. Appearances, too, are deceptive. You may look very safe and respectable on Fifth Avenue, but if you are wearing ninety-cent white ducks and have just changed two wheels or prodded hopelessly inside your greasy engine, you will not look much different from many gangsters and probably less innocent than some. And your exquisite and cultured English accent means little enough in the remoter parts of America and nothing at all to a passing car.

There is also the fact that the hitch hiker is taking as much risk as a car driver, since wicked, designing people are known to travel frequently in cars, offering to give people lifts, and heaven knows what happens to them then.

As a driver, however, you can judge a little by appearances. The over-eager men, or women, but mostly men, who almost allow themselves to be run over in their anxiety to be noticed or who adopt a brutal, threatening attitude are best avoided. Not that the gentle creatures that stand shyly waiting with sorrowful eyes and a half raised hand are always as harmless as they look, but usually the person who points in a matter-of-fact way or jerks his thumb with a hopeful smile is quite safe and probably interesting. If you are interested in people you will find the local countrymen the best value for your generosity. Travelling salesmen are usually dull but have endless funds of stories if you crave this sort of entertainment. College boys can be very pleasant company or they can simply be travelling salesmen in embryo. If you can catch a negro parson down south it's a grand slam and you win, unless your prejudices forbid you to have dealings with the coloured races.

Most of the hitch hikers I have come in contact with have been very polite and have thanked me as they entered and as they were about to leave me, the first time for taking the trouble to stop and the second time for the ride. Some have come and gone without a word of thanks, adopting the attitude that it is the duty of anyone who either owns or is driving a car to pick up and transport free of charge the less fortunate, or perhaps more fortunate ones, who have no car. These ungentle folk, however, are few and far between. As in other countries, the rural people are the most dignified and polite and simple and the college boys, to do them justice, though more elaborate in their thanks, have a charming simplicity of manner and unaffected poise.

If you are very British, you may be of the

I—a

opinion that it is undignified even to suggest that a complete stranger should stop and carry you several miles in his car. In the cities of America, much the same attitude obtains, but in the vast expanses out west and down south, different standards prevail. Anyone you meet is a friend and you expect him to behave as a friend. You talk to him naturally as if you had known him for years. There is no self-consciousness at the beginning nor the cruise mania at the end for exchanging addresses and promising to write, and yet you chat and exchange opinions and experiences as friends. You may never see him again, but while he is there he is important and vital, and if you meet him again you will hail each other with great pleasure and be old friends once more. This friendly attitude is frequently sentimentalized and made to sound mawkish when it is printed in verse on postcards and entitled "Out where the West begins," but there is no denying that it exists.

At all events, what would otherwise be a dull trip across an uninteresting state can be livened up considerably by choosing a companion from the roadside. For those who do not like taking risks of any kind it is wiser and safer to ignore every hitch hiker, however rustic or charming or woebegone. I once drove with a hitch hiker who was being pursued by the police. They followed and claimed him, but he seemed harmless enough.

As for accommodations when driving across country, there are roughly four kinds, hotels, tourist houses, tourist camps and your own camp bed, in order of expense. In the larger eastern cities, you had better stay in hotels, however little margin you may have.

In villages and small towns, you may consider the tourist houses. In fact, you may be forced to consider them, because the only hotel looks so unattractive that you would rather risk a widow in a frame house, for they are mostly widows who keep them, and they are mostly frame houses they keep. If you are driving, it is certainly worth your while to glance at the various tourist houses you see in the residential streets leading down town. Some of them are very pleasant indeed, scrupulously clean, well furnished, and altogether more satisfactory than any hotel in a city of a hundred thousand people or less.

In many you are treated as a guest, and if you care to enjoy a talk with your hostess, she will generally be pleased to oblige. The cost is often no more than a dollar for your room for the night, and the average dollar hotel is a most unsavoury place. However, you must use your judgment. There is usually plenty of choice, especially in mid-western towns. Reputable landladies will always be glad to show you your rooms before you take them, and sometimes the houses are so elegant that you feel that even to glance towards the bed is an insult. Some tourist houses are cathouses in disguise. A cathouse is a kind of brothel. Don't be put off tourist houses, however, on this account, since you are not likely to meet one in five thousand, and if you do, you can just pick up your things and walk out, unless, of course, that is what you were looking for.

As for tourist camps, most of them are unpleasant, and unless you are very hard up, it is better to avoid them. There are some exceptional and charming tourist cabins, with showers attached to your bedroom and a small living-room as well, all costing as much as any moderate hotel, but as a rule the people who stay in cabins do not expect to pay more than fifty or seventy-five cents each. In them you will meet working-class America taking its holidays on the cheap, and plenty of perfectly clean, well-mannered college students and young couples seeing the country. Try one or two, anyway, and decide for yourself. They can be fun, like anything else.

Camping out has its own delights and its own drawbacks. A single camp-bed takes very little room in the rumble seat or on the running board and you usually carry blankets in any car. The procedure in America is much the same as the procedure anywhere else. In the south-west you try to forget the rattlesnakes and other noxious creatures that may bite or sting you into twisted agony or a state of coma at any moment. Many people seem to camp out and very few seem to suffer in any way, except some slight discomfort from the cold. After a hot summer day (it being assumed that you are not camping out in midwinter) the nights are quite cool and it is better to risk an unnecessary blanket or rug or coat than wake up unhappily in the wee hours.

After a few nights of sleeping out you will doubtless long for a real bed and a hot bath, and if you are near a city the meanest hostelry will seem like the Waldorf Astoria. Hotels are cheaper in the west and south, especially in the south in summer. A small town or village may have only one hotel, which may be adequate and may, on the other hand, be very bad indeed.

In the east, and especially in New England, you must learn to distinguish the hotel from the Inn or Tavern. Inns and taverns are full of *objets d'art* and very expensive, the food and accommodation being fair to good. Occasionally you can find one that is a charming old New England house where the food is first class and the rates moderate, but these are

few and far between. The Greylock in Williams-
town, Massachusetts, is an example. It is
spacious and rambling, boasts no "ye ancient
inne" nonsense and is quiet and excellent.
Others, which shall be nameless, charge an
extra dollar per night for every spinning-wheel
in the place, so just count them and see, and
if you think spinning-wheels are cute, by all
means support these little white houses with
decorative signboards. They are quite pretty.

Meals at inns and taverns can be expensive,
and by expensive I mean out of proportion to
the value received. A dinner will be two
dollars, a lunch one dollar and fifty cents and
tea one dollar. For prices, a New England
Inn can put a good London hotel completely
in the shade, and when you consider that a
dollar tea (4/2) is not nearly as satisfactory as
a one and sixpenny British hotel tea as served
in lounges and gardens from Cornwall to
Aberdeen, you can think twice before patroniz-
ing "Ye Olde Taverne." If you find the right
places you can get a perfectly good tea for
thirty-five cents and there is no need to pay
any more. If you pay more than fifty cents
for tea you are encouraging highway robbery.
I may add that if you pay a dollar for your tea,
nothing less than a quarter will do for the
waiter or waitress.

You will need a road map when you drive

in America. Any gas station will give you a map free of charge of the state you, and the gas station, happen to be in. It is good to collect these Sinclair, Texaco and Socony maps and store them in the pocket of your car. If you want a book of road maps covering the entire States you had better buy a Rand McNally Atlas, a handy and bendable book of a hundred pages or so in which first-class roads are clearly marked in red and blue, and other classes of roads in various fancy designs. Eastern Canada is thrown in by way of make-weight and at the end of the book there are plans of about twenty of the largest cities with simply the main streets marked so that you can find your way through and across the crowded sections with speed and comfort. You have only to lose yourself in an unfamiliar city to discover how useful these plans can be.

Just as avenues and streets cut north-south and east-west in New York City, so great transcontinental highways run from Canada south, and from the Atlantic to the Pacific.

These interstate highways are all numbered and there are about a dozen important ones each way. With few exceptions they follow a simple rule. The east-west highways are 10, 20, 30 and so on up to 90, and the north-south highways are 1, 11, 21 and so on up to 101.

Route 10 serves the northern Middle West,

20 connects Boston and Chicago with Yellowstone Park in Wyoming, 30 is the great Lincoln Highway running from Philadelphia through Pittsburgh, Chicago and Cheyenne to Portland, Oregon.

Route 40 serves the Central Middle West and takes you through Indiana, Missouri, Kansas, Colorado and Utah to San Francisco.

Route 50 takes a similar course.

Route 60 connects Virginia, Kentucky, Kansas, Arizona and California.

Route 70, still farther south, runs from North Carolina across Tennessee to El Paso, Texas.

Route 80 is the great southern highway, from Savannah, Georgia, through Louisiana, Texas and Arizona to San Diego, California.

Route 90 starts from Jacksonville, Florida, connects New Orleans with San Antonio and is lost in Western Texas.

In addition to these, routes 2, 6, and 66 are not to be ignored. Route 2 skims the north of the States, crossing Maine, going into Canada, re-entering in the Middle West and reaching Montana. Route 6 begins at the very tip of Cape Cod and ends in Colorado. Route 66 crosses 6 at Chicago and going through Missouri and Oklahoma reaches Los Angeles.

Route 1 runs all the way down the east coast from Maine to Florida, and Route 101 does the same for the west coast.

Route 11 connects Montreal with New Orleans.

Route 21 connects Ohio and Georgia.

Route 31 connects northern Michigan with Alabama.

Route 41 connects northern Wisconsin with Florida.

Route 51 connects northern Wisconsin with Louisiana.

Routes 61 and 71 connect northern Minnesota with Louisiana.

Route 81 connects Winnipeg in Canada with southern Texas and eventually Mexico City.

Route 91 connects Montana with southern California. Out of the series is Route 99 which runs parallel with 101, but east of the coastal range, serving the great fruit-growing San Joaquin Valley of California.

These numbered routes sound prosaic enough, but just drive down one of them and something interesting is sure to happen.

Driving out of New York on Route 1, I had hardly come up for air out of the Holland Tunnel when I was stopped by a police officer. The car I was driving happened to show a Texas license plate. The man asked me whether I was carrying any guns in my car. "No," I said, with a look of innocent surprise.

"You see," he added in explanation, "the last fellow from Texas who drove this way had a machine gun in his rumble seat."

How is maple sugar made?

When is Thanksgiving and what do you eat at it?

What is a Yankee?

What does Winnepesaukee mean?

Who are the Pennsylvania Dutch?

Read Chapter IV, anyway

CHAPTER IV

NEW ENGLAND AND THE EAST

THE East is that part of the United States north of the Mason Dixon line and east of Ohio. To New Englanders the East is just New England and to many city dwellers on the Atlantic coast the East is Boston, New York or Philadelphia.

New England is a general term for most of the country lying east of the Hudson River. There is a strip of New York State immediately east of the river together with New York City and Long Island, and these are not New England. The rest is.

The six New England states are Maine, New Hampshire, Vermont, Massachusetts, Connecticut and Rhode Island. You may, if you like, think of the first three as Northern New England and of the others as Southern New England.

The rest of the East consists simply of the states of New York, New Jersey and Pennsylvania.

If around the city of New Haven, Conneticut, you draw a circle with a hundred miles radius, you enclose New York with its Jersey suburbs, all Long Island, the Hudson valley almost up to Albany, all Connecticut, all but a corner of Rhode Island and about a third of Massachusetts. Over a third of this circle is covered by Atlantic Ocean on which no one has permanent residence. In the other two-thirds lives one-tenth of the entire population of the United States.

Extend your radius to 250 miles and you have over a fifth of the population encircled. So says an advertisement for the New Haven railroad and I have no reason to doubt its statistics.

You would expect the hundred mile circle to be very crowded, and for New York City your guess is right. But an industrial map blackens most of this area covering Southern New England and gives a foreigner the impression that the little squares called Connecticut and Rhode Island, often so small that their names have to be printed out in the Atlantic, are as bleak and dark as they look on the map. On the contrary, the three centuries of colonization in the eastern states have left these states merely dotted with towns and factories. All you have to do is to walk out of a town, or more quickly drive out of one, and you are among the woods and wilds and lonely places in an incredibly short space of time. The motor roads, naturally, have some ribbon development, and you will notice the abrupt end of the town more startlingly if you take some of the trolley cars that run from town to town in Southern New England. They have a habit of turning down little tracks of their own, away from the main roads, and in the Fall you may go miles through flaming red woodland country, crossing an occasional artery and stopping at a small town or two on the way, and this within a few miles of a busy industrial coastal town. You can see the same thing from the railroad between New York, Hartford and Boston.

When a new motor road is built in New England you go for miles without seeing a house until a few weeks or months have elapsed. Then gas stations and restaurants begin to collect along the road and it eventually looks like any other road anywhere else from Ogunquit to Santa Barbara.

In New England you should see its great city, Boston, its universities, Yale and Harvard; its women's colleges, Wellesley, Smith and Mount Holyoke; its prep schools, Exeter and Andover; its smaller cities, Hartford, New Haven, New London, Springfield, Providence and Portland; its villages, Litchfield, Simsbury, Sharon, Guildford, Lyme, Harvard, Deerfield and Provincetown, and its countryside from the Berkshires in the west to Cape Cod in the east, from where Maine drifts into Canada in the north to where Connecticut spills into New York in the south. New England is full and vital. There are schools and colleges all over it, summer resorts on its lakes or on the ocean or up in the hills, and thriving towns with libraries and theatres and concert halls.

A college town has its own atmosphere, and half the towns in New England seem to possess some kind of school or college. There is a campus, neatly criss-crossed with paths, sunny academic buildings, groups of students stringing along the paths, and bells ringing in steeples.

The charm of New England lies in small things and daily happenings. Search for the spirit of New England and you will come away disappointed. Stay in it and its magic will get you, live in it and you will love it for ever.

The winters are long and severe, but between the heavy bouts of rain and the blizzards there are days of brilliant sunshine with a cloudless blue sky and a cold nip in the air. One day the snow will fall thickly and steadily from a grey brown sky, a strange un-American quietness creeps into the streets and parked cars are heaped six inches high with white. And the next is a dazzle of brilliant sun and a tingle of icy wind. Chained tyres whirr along the frozen, glittering roads, and the birds chatter loudly. Even the industrial quarters look cheerful. The coal yards scintillate and the railroad station flaunts its bright metal and the nights are full of trees in the moonlight and brisk cold wind and distant, powdery stars. You crunch through the snow as you walk. The trees bend low over the roads. If you stand by a lake you hear the faint crackling of ice. Your nose is red and your fingers numb. You shuffle your way to the nearest drugstore and eat a ham and egg sandwich and drink coffee.

In the sunlight the white trees outlined against a blue sky look like almond blossom in an English spring. The grass of the college campus or village green is covered and the paths cleanly swept with low little edges of snow, lumpy and uneven.

After a day or two of this crusted glitter, clouds darken the sky to the north. The birds are silent again. A deep plum greyness with no clear beginning to it and apparently no end slides over the mild blue, the sun goes out and it snows again. The steady flakes lick over the smutty caking of old snow, making it white again and soft and edgeless. Windows are lighted early in the afternoon and stand out small and glowing like little squares of moving life. The twigs are shapeless with snow. The

K—a

strange quietness steals over everything once more. There are voices but no footsteps, the chugging of engines but no wheels. The last clear noise of the road is an occasional whizz of chains or the roar of a far-off trolley-car.

Even in New England, however, the snow goes the way of all snow and thaws in the chilliest and messiest manner imaginable. Don't let your first visit to New England be during a thaw, unless it happens to be Northern New England during the great and final thaw of the oncoming spring. There is something beautiful in that. But the miserable, slushy thaws of the southern towns and villages reveal no subtleties of sight or smell or hearing or feeling.

It was in the spring that I drove through New England into Canada. We decided to go north on the west side of Lake Champlain and to return through Vermont, on the east side of the lake.

We reached Amherst only the first evening because we paid two lengthy calls, one lasting most of the morning and early afternoon at Holyoke, during which we saw, and heard, some of the loveliest old harpsichords in America, and the other at South Hadley.

It was evening by the time we reached Amherst, which is a quiet little college town in Massachusetts. It is in rolling country over-

looking miles of sweeping wooded valley with
hills beyond in lines of green, purple and blue.
Some of the trees were still brownish gold,
others were sprouting a faint green. The pines
only were a rich, full colour. It was a warm
and springlike evening but in the shadows
there was still a little snow. It was the fifth of
April.

When we arrived I called at the post office,
and a man hearing I was a stranger to Amherst
asked me where I came from and whether I
was on holiday. I told him that two of us from
college were driving to Canada in one small
car and were staying the night at Amherst.
With a kind of friendly diffidence he suggested
that we should stay at his house for about half
the rates usually charged at hotels. He said
we could go on our own and look at it anyway,
so that we needn't feel obliged to come unless
we wanted to, but there it was if we wanted it.
He was a matter-of-fact and kindly New Eng-
lander offering a favour with a take-it-if-you-
want air. We looked at the house and liked it.
It was small and pleasantly furnished. It was
far back from the road and the birds sang very
lustily in the trees. The charge was a dollar
for the night for each of us. The good man and
his wife approached us after supper and said,
"You won't mind us going out to-night, will
you? You can have the whole house to your-

selves and there's plenty of wood for the fire."

That is typical of New England and of the Yankee character. Yankees are not, as many English people imagine, all Americans, but only New Englanders. Indeed, if your English accent is non-committal, you may find southerners and westerners calling you a Yankee when they see the Connecticut or Massachusetts license plate on your car. They will not be far wrong, for the derivation of the word Yankee is as likely to be the French "anglais" as anything else, though many suggestions have been put forward.

New Englanders are shrewd and business-like, with bright, honest eyes, humorous mouths and sharp chins. Some of the country people have the hook noses of the fen district, a dry, nasal speech, a kind, unsentimental bearing, and a rural pride and dignity.

The next day we cut across a corner of Vermont on our way towards the Adirondacks in New York State, or rather we tried to cut across a corner of Vermont. We took what looked like a short cut on the map. It turned out to be a third-class road in the spring thaw of Vermont, and that makes it tenth class, no less. It deceived us amiably by improving in patches and then plunging us into a slope of moving mud. The car came to a groaning, hot and smelly standstill, and the wheels whirled around in the snow and mud and beat the two into a treacle that climbed gradually towards the axles.

About half an hour of prodding and levering with a long pole, we managed to shove the car back on to a dry piece of road, and after that we turned and drove back to the main road in Massachusetts and so into New York State. Even the main roads were slippery with ice and occasionally flooded, and in one place, where they were doing repairs, so muddy that we once more found ourselves stuck and had to be hauled out by a truck. The roads which ran between a slope and a dip were streaming with icy water and the air echoed with the tinkle of the general melting. All the lakes were frozen and in the north the rivers as well. The sheltered woods were still thick with snow, and the mist drifted off the lakes and hung around the trees. Along the slushy little Vermont lane, each maple tree had one, two, three or four buckets hanging on to it, about four feet from the ground, and as the snows melted in the sun, the sap rose in the trees and the clear, transparent syrup dropped slowly into the buckets. Down near the farms and dwellings were the little sugar-boiling houses where the thin pale fluid thickened to a golden syrup and finally crystallized into a light brown sugar.

Vermont in summer is a very different place. Its Green Mountains are green, the air is scented with the heat of the sun on the pines, and sharp thunder-showers hiss among the trees and on the roofs.

Summer comes quickly in New England and the trees lose their spring delicacy early. Hedges flaunt yellow, pink and white in huge and showy sprays. City workers look hot and tired, and the more fortunate go north or east to the mountains or the shore. Beaches and islands are crowded with bathers, and the green and golden coast is busy from Connecticut on Long Island Sound to the easternmost coves of Maine.

If you are in New England in the summer you should avoid the towns. Remember that Boston is on the same latitude as central Italy. While the city sidewalks are sweltering in ninety degrees, the upstate villages are cool and green and the lake water is actually cold.

To the northwest of Connecticut and the west of Massachusetts are the Berkshires, lovely rolling country with inns and golf courses and rivers and summer theatres in plenty. Vermont and New Hampshire have the Green Mountains and the White Mountains respectively. All the New England states have ocean beaches except Vermont, which has the entire length of Lake Champlain instead. All have lakes and forests, and Massachusetts has a special treasure in Cape Cod, the Cornwall of North America.

All this country is lovely in the summer, but it is exquisite in the Fall.

My first visit to northern New England was in October, when the Fall is at its height, or, if the locution offends the purists, at its most intense. It was New Hampshire I was visiting, and New Hampshire is well named. It is all one beautiful forest with occasional farms and grassy slopes, sudden views of distant hills, the White Mountains to the north, white wooden houses standing far back from the roads, and twisted wooded lanes now thick with fallen leaves and acorns. Add to all this a scattering of old country people, the colours of the Fall, a clear blue sky, a warm sun and a whistling wind, and you have New Hampshire as I first saw it.

It is about three hundred and fifty miles from New York, a day's ride in the train or a day's automobile drive, since the roads are good in New England and once you are out of the New York area there is nothing to hold back your speed.

As you go by train through Connecticut, Rhode Island and Massachusetts, you catch glimpses of the water in Long Island Sound, you cross great rivers that sweep around magnificent curves towards the sea, blue and silver curves thickly lined with green and yellow trees, and of inland woods, red and orange, brown and yellow, every colour that sings the end of the summer and the coming of the Fall.

Steaming northwards at sunset with lakes and rivers and woods on either side and the feel of the evening, the smell of the trees and the tang of the chilly air, I had the dark blue east on my right and the glowing yellow west lingering on the surface of the water we passed on the left. The slow transition from blue to yellow was over our heads but I could see nothing but darkness on my right and brightness on my left. It was like skimming along between night and day. Some of the little stations were lit with oil lamps, graceful yellow flickering things nailed to the wooden slats of the wall. They reminded me of Anglesey where the yellow oil lamps still burn on the line to Holyhead.

I was met at Franklin, N.H., and driven some twenty miles through pitch black woods, up and down, round corners with the trees all flat like scenery in the headlights of the car. It was dark and lonely and beautiful. At last we came to the school at which I was to stay. It dominated a tiny village among the woods. The school was a line of houses, some brick, some white wood, set apart among lawns and trees, now dusted over with the fallen leaves. It was lovely by night, but still lovelier by day with the copper leaves burning against the white wood and the blue sky, the falling leaves flying down to the already crowded grass, and the green slopes of the school fields stretching beyond up to the forests themselves. On the sunny smooth slopes at the edge of the playing-fields were clumps of blazing, flaming maple trees, each with its carpet of shed leaves under it, and all alight in the glow of the sun. When evening came it grew cold in less than an hour and the wind whistled down from the snowy mountains. The snug, heated houses were very welcome at night.

The day after my arrival we drove a dozen miles or so to a small town for lunch, and saw, from a high part of the road, lake Winnepesaukee (the Smile of the Great Spirit) among the trees, a little sullen because the sun had gone behind a cloud, but usually glittering to the sky like other New England lakes, satisfied and happy with the beauty of the long lake set among the scarlet trees and the solemn formal pines.

That night I took a walk alone down the road that led out of the village. After passing a few white houses, rosy with light at the windows, I found myself on a road winding among the trees as if it were wriggling to throw me off its back. It was quite dark and the wind was tearing through the trees and blowing the leaves along the surface of the road behind me. It sounded like the scratching of tiny horned feet and hands as if goblins were hurrying in a wild and helter-skelter chase along the road. I got home again just as it was beginning to rain. In two minutes the rain was pelting down and I heard thunder echoing among the hills. Then it was colder still and dry, and the wind dropped and it was starry.

Next day I strolled seven miles along a dusty, maple-lined road that climbed hills and twisted and sloped down and was thick with acorns and red leaves, full of the dusty sweetness of late summer.

New England is quiet and rich and golden, with nothing foreign about it at all. It smacks of the Hampshire woods, the New Forest, of Warwickshire lanes, and there are glimpses of Surrey and Hertfordshire and Bedfordshire and even an occasional touch of Wales. It's not a country to be homesick in, not a country of olives and low blazing stars and liquid language. The trees are elms and birches, pines, firs, maples and larches, the stars are like the stars of England, a little brighter perhaps, but faintly powdered, high and withdrawn; and the language is a deep burr, dry and nasal, redolent of the soil, of golden fields at harvest and of apple orchards. It isn't foreign. It's as native as the core of Sussex or Somerset or Buckinghamshire. It's a place with an abiding, gentle beauty, a rich, healthy smell, familiar, lovable folks and a sturdy British soul.

The names are English, Maple Lawn Farm, Sleepy Hollow, Red Gables, Sunrise Farm, Willowbrook Tavern, Pine Island House, Bay Cottage. When the names are foreign, they are so undisguised and fantastic that you feel that they were there before any people at all and that they just belong to the age old hills and streams—Sunapee, Waubanaki, Wawbeek, Keokuk, Passumpsic, Neshobe, Wyoda, Beenadeewin and Quinebeck. In their softness and perky humour they are not unlike the Celtic names that would have been all over Britain if the English had been content to stay on the Continent, names like Tonypandy in Wales, Killiecrankie in Scotland, Kilkee in Ireland and Bannalec in Brittany.

One Saturday night in the Fall, October 21st to be exact, I was driving to Connecticut from Vermont. I wanted to buy some Vermont maple sugar to send to England and I wanted to buy it in Vermont so that I could truthfully say it came from the maple sugar state. Five or six miles north of the Massachusetts state line I found a house that sold it. It was white and small and very dark, so dark that we nearly fell over things trying to find the door. Inside the house three men were sitting and playing musical instruments of ancient vintage. We waited until the end of the jolly little country dance they were playing before we tapped at the door and disturbed them.

The owner put down his fiddle when we told him what we wanted and poked around in a chilly storeroom while the other two smiled shyly and fingered their instruments. After few words, for Vermonters are silent folk, we took our little boxes, on the lid of which was a picture of the buckets hanging on the trees catching the sap in the spring and the boiling house near by. Then we said good-night and went. As we stumbled back to the road in the dark, the three musicians burst into a merry tune that sounded like an old jig. We drove on, thinking how pleasant and rural it all was, and how unlike the average Englishman's conception of Americans and their Saturday nights.

The next day, Sunday, we bought bunches of the flame-coloured bittersweet that grows on the Connecticut hills, and a large jar of cherry cider. Sunday morning was English, not New English at all. It was a midland autumn morning, Warwickshire perhaps, grey and still and rural, with cows standing in the fields and not a yellow leaf falling from the heavy trees.

Later on the sun came out and the wind rose. You feel that in New England the leaves should be dancing the whole time in the wild sunlight and the roads should be thick with skeltering leaves, and the trees should snow them down fluttering in the light and wind. The Fall is so splendid and triumphant that there is no time to be sad and still. They burn leaves in great heaps by the side of the village roads, but the atmosphere is one of moving life, and the white houses stand back on their wide green lawns and smile. There is crackling in the woods and a tang of snow in the air.

Every farmhouse on the road and many little cabins and shanties have trestles outside in full view of passing cars, the boards all stacked with glowing pumpkins and other autumn fruit. Underneath the tables are baskets of the same fruit and kegs of sweet apple cider.

In New England you have only to get away from the concrete roads and gas stations to imagine yourself in the eighteenth century. The village greens and the pure white churches, the neat square windows and the lawns dotted with trees are like the old lithographs in their precision and contrast.

New England has wildness and serenity, snow and sunshine, rich foliage and the lacery of winter bareness, colour in the Fall, green in the summer, dead black and fierce white in the winter. The houses are dignified, clean and square.

Even as late as November, New England weather is often mild and pleasant. I have climbed a rock overlooking Long Island Sound on a sparkling November afternoon, the trees and fields below, orange, scarlet and green, and beyond, the silver Sound, gleaming long and flat and cool, and on the horizon the cold grey edge of Long Island. When the red sun dips into the west it quickly grows cold and even in the brilliance of noonday there is a suspicion of a sharp tang in the air waiting for the sun to hide.

The great national feast and holiday of Thanksgiving is held on the last Thursday in November. For some reason, this feast is made more of in New England than elsewhere, partly for historic reasons and partly perhaps because Vermont is famous for turkeys, and turkeys are eaten in millions on Thanksgiving Day in America.

On this day you eat your turkey with cranberry sauce, followed by pumpkin pie and sweet cider. I ate my first Thanksgiving Dinner with a New England family. It happened not to be one of the mild November days, but a snowy one. The fields and woods were covered with snow. The sky was a deep sullen grey and as it grew dark, the farmhouses, all white and snowy, glowed with rosy lights in the square windows and little fir trees stood proud and erect in front of them, heavy with snow. Little black streams, unfrozen, tinkled merrily between white banks, and all the time the snow floated down among the trees and gradually settled.

In addition to the turkey and its "fixings" there was bean porridge and clam chowder and johnny cake, and I was given real New England maple syrup and a precious dish of maple sugar crystallized twelve years ago. The grandmother told me all about the farm her folks had upstate, and how she used to help her mother with the syrup gathering and the sugaring. They used to cut spigots of sumach, stick them in holes in the trees, and hang cans below, and the maple syrup used to drip out like water, thin and colourless and only faintly sweet. Then they used to boil it three or four times, and at last they would get the real thick syrup, and finally sugar.

The kind of sumach they used (generally pronounced "shoemack") must have been some harmless kind, since the poison ivy variety cannot be touched without painful results. It grows widely in woods and hedges all over the States, and once pointed out can be remembered by its appearance and avoided.

It has little white flowers and small whitish-yellow berries.

Thanksgiving is primarily a religious festival like Christmas Day and it dates from 1621 when the Pilgrim Fathers landed safely on the shores of New England. Since 1864 the last Thursday in November has been set apart for this festival and the people are not only grateful for their country's foundation but also for the things the British are thankful for at Harvest Thanksgiving, held on various Sundays throughout the British Isles.

New England town churches not only on such occasions as Thanksgiving and Christmas Day but usually every Sunday, compete with each other in playing different hymn tunes on their peals of bells.

The concert generally takes place at six o'clock, when you are eating your evening meal. As you finish your clam chowder one bell begins, brightly tolling "Now the Day is Over"; another instantly chimes in with "The King of Love my Shepherd is" a minor third higher, while as you tackle your chicken and waffle, a third mournfully peals "Abide with Me," a semitone off one of the other keys. Other and smaller churches, not aspiring to whole hymns, jealously clang all their bells haphazard so as to ruin whatever effect the three principal churches might achieve. The churches have apparently realized that modesty, though a Christian virtue, does not fill the collection plate.

There is a prejudice in New England against other parts of the east. When I announced in a New England house that I was going on a trip into New Jersey and Pennsylvania they said "How dreadful!" and asked why.

The three eastern states not included in New England are New York, New Jersey and Pennsylvania.

New York State is rather more than New York City. It is over three hundred miles long and over three hundred miles broad. Manhattan and Long Island look like a little appendix tucked away at one corner as if there were no room for Long Island without its having to squeeze itself along the Connecticut coast in a neglected sort of way.

In addition to important cities like Albany, Buffalo, Rochester and Syracuse, New York State has vast tracts of wild and beautiful country, mostly formed into State parks. The Hudson valley itself is beautiful and very near New York. The Albany Night Line boats will take you up and down the river and you can drive along highways on either bank.

Lake Champlain separates the north-eastern part of the State from Vermont and the north-western border fronts the Saint Lawrence

L—a

river, Lake Ontario and part of Lake Erie,
with the famous Niagara Falls just between
those two lakes. Part of the southern border
follows the Delaware River, with its lovely
water gap, as it is called. The beauty spots of
New York State, however, are not primarily on
these lake and river borders.

The centre of the State, in the west, is called
the Finger Lake region, and a glance at the
map will tell you why. Leading to this region
from the eastern part of the State is the
Mohawk trail, now a first class highway, and
it is from this trail that you see the nearest
thing to the great West without going a morning's journey from New York.

South of the Mohawk trail are the Catskills,
a cluster of low mountains, and to the north
a mountainous, forested region full of lakes
and rivers called the Adirondacks.

Pennsylvania is almost as large as New York
and spreads itself in a thick rectangle between
the Delaware River and Lake Erie. Its
southern boundary is the Mason Dixon line
which marks the division between the North
and the South. Philadelphia in the east is two
hours' drive from New York. Pittsburgh on
the other side of the State is almost in the
Middle West. Across Lake Erie is Canada.
Over the Mason Dixon line is the South.

Pennsylvania might boast of being the core

of eastern North America. Its eastern rivers,
the Susquehanna and the Delaware, drain into
the Atlantic Ocean. Lake Erie washes forty
miles of Pennsylvania shore on its way to the
Gulf of Saint Lawrence, between Canada and
Newfoundland. And the Ohio River, which
begins in Pennsylvania at the junction of the
Monongahela and the Allegheny, joins the
Mississippi at Cairo and carries the Pennsylvania mountain rains to the Gulf of Mexico.

Any map of Pennsylvania is full of names,
but don't be misled into thinking that there is
no country in Pennsylvania. The Allegheny
Mountains stretch across the State in great,
forested ridges. In some of the valleys are coal
mines and industrial cities, but almost pouring
into the city streets are miles of wild forest land,
not only among the Alleghenies but west
towards Pittsburgh, about twelve million acres
altogether, no mean stretch for a State that
ranks first in mineral industries and second in
population in the entire Union.

Philadelphia, on the Delaware, is a fine city
with parks and boulevards and sky-scrapers and
one of the best Symphony Orchestras in the
world, its American rivals being both on the
Atlantic coast, the Boston Symphony and the
New York Philharmonic. Like Boston and
New York, Philadelphia has its social and cul-
tural life and you must stay there some while

before you really know the city or you will know it only as I know it, very slightly, but admiringly, and saving it up for a future occasion.

Between Philadelphia and the highest ridge of the Alleghenies lies the home of the Pennsylvania Dutch, who are not Dutch at all, but German in origin. Their German dialect is as different from Heidelberg German as Virginian from Cambridge English. Their American speech is coloured with a sing song intonation not unlike the English spoken by some Welsh people and they are sometimes very difficult to understand. They are great singers and beer drinkers and their towns are Allentown, Bethlehem, Reading, Lebanon and Harrisburg, and a host of almost pure German villages with names like Grimville, Fritztown and Werners, the -ville suffix being very common indeed in this region.

The country is wild and forested, and parts of it resemble southern Germany. I was there twice, both times in the early spring. The roads were bad and it was snowy but sunny. We drove and walked in the country near Kutztown. As it grew dark we passed strange, lonely little villages with German names, tiny general stores and oil lamps shining yellowly in the windows. One man we spoke to had a round German face glowing with health, smiling blue eyes and fair Nordic hair. Another could hardly speak a word of English.

Driving from Kutztown to Philadelphia, a fine rain fell and froze instantly on the windshield, so that I had to scrape the ice off every five minutes and the automatic wiper was quite useless. At last it became so persistent that I just hung out of the window in the freezing drizzle and drove the last twenty miles in that position. I noticed some people with burning candles fixed to their windshields to melt the ice and make driving easier.

I hope that particular experience is not typical of Pennsylvania. The second time I was in the State on my way to South Carolina I was caught in a fierce blizzard, but in the summer Pennsylvania is hot and the summer resorts in the mountains are pleasant and mild, though the inland waters are only one-fifth the extent they are in New York State.

The Germans are not the only Europeans who settled in Pennsylvania. English Quakers settled there, and any school or college list will show Poles and Italians and Irish. Scranton and Wilkes Barre are strong Welsh colonies.

New Jersey is a twisted little State lying between the Delaware River and the ocean, a businesslike piece of country of some eight thousand square miles. It houses a third of New York City's commuters, the other two-thirds living in New York State either on the mainland or on Long Island. Opposite Manhattan and New York Bay crowd Jersey City, Bayonne, Newark and Elizabeth, manufacturing centres, and over the river from Philadelphia sits Camden. In this respect New Jersey seems to be a state of backdoors, but it has its own capital of Trenton which, in its residential district along the bank of the Delaware river, is very pleasant.

The sea coast is more than a hundred miles long and is one long chain of seaside resorts from Sandy Hook to Cape May.

Apart from suburbs and boardwalks and manufacturing towns, however, there is a rural New Jersey, wooded and hilly in the Kittitinny Mountains to the north-west of the State, and gently rolling in the central part.

I stayed in a white frame manse in a New Jersey village, not more than fifty miles from New York City. To drive there from New York in little more than an hour is an experience, and if you dislike New York, a refreshing experience. If your vision of the city is one of hurrying crowds, bleating taxis, roaring trains, badly painted women, greasy little men yapping Italian and Yiddish, reckless spending, piteous whining for a nickel, harsh laughter, cruel eyes, hardness, godlessness, blazing lights and multitudes of crawling human bodies in a mad struggle for existence, you will find New Jersey, and especially a New Jersey manse, safe and pleasant.   There is a farm nearby where you can go for eggs and buttermilk. Countrywomen calling to see the parson's wife will sit on a kitchen chair and tell you how the great blizzard almost smothered their cottages and how they cut their way through the snow to save the farm animals. If you are very fortunate you may meet Mrs. Reilly, a little brown-faced woman of seventy or more who will probably announce brightly, "I'm not ashamed of my age like some folks. The Lord has let me live to this age and I'm glad to be about and able."

On the edge of the village was a large old house with a living-room like a barn. I went visiting there one night. There was a log fire on the hearth and an oil lamp on the table. From the wall frowned two heavy portraits in gold frames and we all sat in rocking chairs and talked in the dim glow. Outside it was cold and misty. The little village seemed so kind and quiet. I visited its tiny school where an embarrassed looking hen and a weakly corn-stalk were the afternoon subjects for nature study. I spent hours sitting on the porch looking out over the sunny fields to the hills beyond. The rhythm of the village was of a beat with that of a Kentish hamlet fifty miles from London.

Do you know what Mother's Day is?

Do you know the vulgar English for cuspidor, School of Cosmetology, pantorium and de-hairolysis?

Do you avoid restaurants called Taste Rite and Do Drop In?

Do you know how to make good coffee?

Do you know how to make a mint julep?

Do you know the tunes of "Jingle Bells," "East Side, West Side," and "She'll be comin' round the mountain"?

You should. Read Chapter V.

CHAPTER V

THE AMERICAN PEOPLE

THERE is no greater barrier between two
people, or peoples, than a different approach
to humour. Many Americans are quite con-
vinced that no Englishman has any sense of
humour whatever. On the other hand an
intelligent and witty Englishman is frequently
bored by having to smile at an American joke
which is so obvious as to be painful. It is true,
I think, to say that the average Englishman
either sees through an American joke too
quickly or never sees through it at all. An
American joke is usually a mental short cut,
and the Englishman rarely arrives at the
exact psychological moment that makes it
funny. American humour is right angled.
Your short cut is away from the apparent line
of mental progress. Some of the most exquisitely
amusing jokes in the *New Yorker* are of this
kind. To read *Punch* after reading the *New
Yorker* regularly is to find it as deadly and
bewildering as the *New Yorker* itself seemed on
first reading. Over-elaboration seems to be

the fault of the English joke. When an English joke is good, it is a beautifully conceived piece of subtlety. Inferior jokes are clumsy and unsuccessful, but none the less well meant strivings after subtlety. American jokes are hit or miss. When they are good they are brilliant and it is hard to say exactly why. When they are bad they just hurt.

All this refers only to humour published for human consumption and the people, large masses of them on both sides of the Atlantic, who base their standards of humour entirely on such publication and have no individual trends of their own. Individual people, however, exist in both countries, and there is always closer kinship between these whatever their origin than between the individual and the mass in any one country.

An American and an Englishman can together find humour in an unsuspecting American or unsuspecting Englishman, but the mass has necessarily few points of contact, and difference of idiom baffles it completely and for all time. An American may try to set you at your ease by saying "Sarah Mony is out for the evening" and then elaborately explain what you have already guessed, that Sarah Mony is merely "ceremony," pronounced in American fashion. If you are quick-witted you will see that before it comes and be impressed only by its stupidity, and if you are slow-witted you will not see it at all, but you will probably have a similar "ham" phrase up your own sleeve which will leave the dull-witted American equally nonplussed.

There is, of course, ground which is peculiar to each country and foreign to the other. It indicates a dull wit on the part of the American who bases his assumption that the English cannot see a joke on the fact that an Englishman untravelled in America did not laugh at a pictorial story featuring a travelling salesman or a midwestern Women's Club. Just as it indicates a dull wit on the part of the Englishman who ridicules the American who does not laugh at the menu phrase commonly seen in American restaurants "Combinations cannot be changed." If you happen to have been brought up in a country where, when you see the word "combination" you think of under-clothing, it is natural to be startled and amused at the incongruity of its appearance on a menu. But you cannot expect an American to have the same outlook. Similarly, travelling salesmen to an Englishman do not conjure up a whole host of stories and associations. The term itself is foreign. Even if you translate quickly to "commercial traveller" the concep·tion is different.

These barriers of idiom, however, are simply

ones of habit of thought. You can, after a while, adapt yourself to a habit of thought, especially if you associate with foreign people and are seldom given the opportunity of falling back on your basic habits of thought, which, if you are British, will be British.

Assuming that barrier broken down the next will doubtless be a question of Central Heating. If you are accustomed to cold baths, airy rooms, coal fires, and your bedroom window open at night, you will find American houses hot and stuffy, and the Americans unusually fussy about draughts and open windows. When you grow accustomed to the high indoor temperatures you will see things from their point of view, especially if you have to endure an icy British bedroom after a cosy American indoor winter.

You will probably like their houses. Rooms often open into other rooms without any fussy doors, and with Central Heating, there are no draughts. I refer, of course, to downstairs rooms. Bedrooms and bathrooms have doors. Wood is plentiful, and floors are usually of plain wood with a few rugs here and there. Lighting is attractive. Instead of the deadly centre light with its weak glare so popular in suburban England, American houses have several small shaded lamps, table lamps, bridge lamps and so on, giving the room a pleasant contrast of glow and shadow instead of the pale depressing whiteness that invariably comes from one badly shielded light source.

The living room usually has a fireplace and logs are burnt, not primarily for warmth but simply because a log fire looks attractive. The steam heating apparatus is concealed except in small and primitive houses.

During my first few weeks in America, sitting by a log fire in an already well heated room with all the windows shut sent me almost to sleep by eight o'clock, but I became accustomed to it in time.

The natural heat in the summer and the artificial heat in the winter make the possession of an ice box or electric refrigerator a necessity in America. For the ice box you have to buy ice regularly from the ice man, who is generally the local coal man as well. For the refrigerator you buy nothing except the refrigerator itself, which is why so many young couples go on buying ice.

The Americans seem to suffer widely from sinus trouble, and the heat and dryness of their houses may have something to do with this. Their complexions are certainly paler and tougher than the British, but where they lose in natural colour they gain in texture. Their skins are for the most part smooth and soft, like chamois leather, and seldom have the rough redness often observed in England. They take great care of them and show sunburn beautifully.

The Americans are cleaner, inside and out, than the British. Their plumbing is more advanced, they bathe more frequently, and they study their diet. They drink water (ice water) at almost every meal, adults drink quantities of milk and orange juice, and they eat plenty of salads and fruit.

Their teeth are far better than the teeth in Britain. Their dentistry is excellent and expensive. They are trained early to use dental floss and to have their mouths frequently examined. Good teeth are the rule rather than the exception in America, whereas good teeth are very definitely the exception in Britain, especially in Wales and Scotland.

The Americans walk far less than the British, and there is a tendency for the development of the top-heavy type of well built man, with immense shoulders and arms, medium, not very small waist and long, slim legs. This type is common among the undergraduates at the large eastern universities. The women tend to medium shoulders, long waists, smooth hiplines and slim arms and legs. There are, of course, national types, but the "typical" young Americans seem to be predominantly of the kind described.

On the question of walking, the average American walks very little. A friend of mine in Hollywood who was taking me around Los Angeles asked me whether I minded four or five blocks to a café. I said no, and told him that one evening I had walked home to my hotel from the Theatre Mart because I liked to walk and it was a pleasant evening. He was astonished. It was miles, he said. Actually, it was forty-five minutes' easy walking. I did not tell him that I had also walked there.

One night, having booked a ticket for a song recital in the Greek Theatre, Griffith Park, Hollywood, and having nothing to do immediately before it, I walked about a mile and a half to it. It was a beautiful, fresh evening, and my walk took me along an avenue in the park that led directly to the theatre, but I saw no one on the way there nor on the way back, that is, no one on foot. I saw many cars, and when I arrived at the theatre I found a parking ground full of them, and one or two special buses for the minority without cars. The theatre is an open air one and you dress informally, but to no one except myself, apparently, had the idea of walking occurred.

I knew a girl in the east who waited a week to be driven down town because it was too far to walk. Down town is just a quarter or

M—a

half a mile away and across a pleasant college campus and a New England town green. Another girl in the same town invited me to tea and apologized for living four blocks up the street. However, she added, there was a trolley car.

I have actually been with Americans who have walked farther and wasted more time going to a parked car, driving three blocks and then finding difficulty in parking again, than the distance and time involved in walking three blocks and back.

Even the people who have no cars do the same with trolley cars and buses. If you ask the way anywhere in an American city, an obliging person will instantly tell you the number or letter of the car or bus that will take you there. Ask him how far it is and when he has recovered from his surprise that you want to walk, he will tell you that it is all of six or seven city blocks, just fifteen minutes' walk.

Yet some Americans walk and they are not hard to find. The impression of the non-walking American is conveyed not so much by the overwhelming majority of non-walkers, but by the extreme aversion to walking shown by that majority. Many Americans walk, but they are not so noisy about it as the non-walkers are about not wanting to walk. In Britain it is the other way round. It is the walkers who are more noisy.

Country people in America walk considerably. So do hitch hikers of all kinds when they are not riding in other people's cars. I knew an undergraduate who would tramp the woods with me for hours. I also knew a charming Rhode Island girl who often asked other Americans to walk with her and frequently went alone because the other young men and women preferred driving or staying at home.

College Americans, though they walk comparatively little, make up for it by taking more violent and more artificial exercise. They do plenty of swimming and take it quite seriously. In the college pools they learn to crawl by swimming patiently up and down holding on to floating boards. There is no levity, either in the pool or in the other rooms of the gymnasium where you may find droves of young Americans learning simple athletics and earnestly doing body building exercises.

If you are invited to swim in an American men's college pool, don't expect to be allowed to wear anything. You go nudist in these places and you take the necessary showers before entering the water. And if you happen in some midwestern town to go into the Y.M.C.A. swimming pool, often the only one in town, the same procedure obtains, and don't be offended if you are offered a piece of soap. It is not a personal insult but a health regulation. Take it and use it.

It will cost you a dollar to swim in an hotel pool unless you are an hotel guest. The main New York pools are at the Shelton and Park Central hotels. If you like to cross over to Brooklyn you can swim in the magnificent Saint George Hotel pool. It and the Yale pool in New Haven are the most famous swimming pools in America.

Health regulations are strict in America, and some colleges require an annual physical examination of every student. Even mental health received some attention until recently, but students took such joy in pleading guilty to the most startling excesses that any serious study of it was impossible.

A girl at one college told me that lady doctors had no sense of humour and supported her generalization by saying that she had gone to be examined and a severe matron had stood her against a wall and ordered her to put up both her arms and turn her head to one side.

"Shall I smile?" asked the girl.

"It doesn't make any difference," snapped the lady doctor.

There is an idea among English people that the standard of morality among young people is lower in America than in Britain, and to judge from observation, the idea would seem not to be unfounded. A searching of high school lockers by teachers in some eastern cities has shed considerable light on the lives that are led by some of the sixteen year olds of America.

Nor can the Middle West or the West cast the first stone at the East. I was told by a Middle Westerner that in his home town the wildest young people were the high school boys and girls. When, at the age of eighteen or nineteen they went to college, they settled down and became staidly middle-aged. That may be an exaggeration, but it is true that, as in some continental countries, young people mature earlier in America. Some of the high school children, especially the girls, look at least twenty, and I have seen some that would pass for thirty.

American high school girls do not wear gym tunics or school hats, and there are few rosy cheeks or athletic figures among them. Some are of stunted growth, over-mature, dark and Latin looking, with swarthy complexions, or thin and pale, with bleached hair. Many of them make up heavily and wear cheaply fashionable hats, quantities of jewelry and fur coats. They carry their books crooked in one arm, femininely and fascinatingly. I seldom saw one romp or forget the grown-up part she was playing. That is only true of an industrial city and of the class that will eventually work in shops and restaurants and dowdy offices.

On the other hand, some of the high school girls, and some of the boys as well, were polite and self assured, and impressed me with their mental maturity and poise. They seemed to have lost the noisy assertiveness of the average American child, escaped the vulgarity of their associates and retained only a rather attractive naïve sophistication. Many of them never seemed to have experienced the awkward stage and the boys were not clumsy nor the girls giggly.

Generally speaking, the young men were mentally behind the young women of school and undergraduate age. The absence of affectation which is so refreshing in most young Americans seemed simply gaucherie in the early twenties. The average undergraduate is a pleasant fellow, courteous and warmly distant, and you feel that he is happiest when he is sinking his individuality with "a bunch of good fellows." Intelligent or individual young college men in America have a hard time. I knew several perfectly normal, healthy young men who were not admitted to these bunches of good fellows because they dared to confess an interest in music or art. The young American male is so afraid of oddness or pretentiousness that a sincere desire to appreciate what is good and be able to distinguish it from what is bad is enough to damn one in the eyes of the mass. Like children, young Americans can be very cruel to the individual.

The women are more precocious than the men. A young Vassar woman of seventeen told me that she and her friends invariably found it necessary to talk down to men two or three years their senior, and this seemed to me no exaggeration. There are, of course, many thousands of stupid women in America, but the average college girl is as intelligent as she is charming. She is occasionally spoilt, but nevertheless charming.

America is still a woman's country and the men are still merely adoring wage earners, but only half the people really act on that impression. It is true that labour-saving devices together with favourable climatic conditions have made the care of a house not a very arduous business in America even for the woman who has no servant. Women who in this country would have hired assistance and still find little time for leisure do without a maid in America and have enough time on their hands to belong to clubs and enjoy life.

The standard of living in America is higher than in Britain. No household is complete without at least one car, a radio, and a refrigerator, and people who in Britain would never aspire to these luxuries, except the standard cheap radio, regard them as absolute necessities in America.

A lady who worked for charity in Saint Paul told me that they had to take away the license plates of those people who accepted charity in the way of groceries from them, to prevent these destitute wretches from using their cars. One man refused to give up his license, even though the organization offered to give him trolley car checks.

A doctor in Minneapolis told me that a negro boy was brought to a free clinic in the city by his father in a magnificent limousine, the car being the property of the father, not someone else's car being driven by him.

However, there was recent mention in a New York magazine of English people who drove up to Labour Exchanges in taxis to draw their unemployment benefits, so the Americans probably have the same opinion of us.

Admitting the possibility of our own share of shiftlessness and extravagance, it is fair to say that American middle class life is a good deal less safe than British, and seems to be based on the *carpe diem* theory. "Gather ye rosebuds while ye may" sang Herrick while America was being busily colonized, and now, two centuries and a half later, the Americans are

gathering rosebuds while they may and sometimes while they mayn't. Many middle class
people have mortgaged their houses in order
to possess cars and refrigerators, and some of
them seem to be consumed with a desire to
live well beyond their means. After all, there
is some excitement in living on the edge of a
volcano, especially when it erupts and burns
someone who lives a mile away and leaves
you unhurt. In the bank crashes of 1931-1933
it was the people who had saved their money
who suffered most.

There is little of the air of permanence about
Americans. At any moment they might go
and live in some other state, even though they
have lived in their home state for forty or
fifty years. Their houses lack that settled,
built-in quality of an English home, and their
gardens are mostly dumps. It is as if they
were never sure whether they would be there
next week. And if you might be moving on,
why clean up and plant a garden? Someone
else may come and enjoy it.

If the Americans are not generous towards
posterity, they are open handed enough towards
their contemporaries. They grow comparatively few beautiful gardens, but such as they are
—and a simple well trimmed lawn with a
reddening maple tree on it can be very satisfying—they share with the rest of the world.

Their gardens are not walled or fenced or jealously guarded. They lie open to the road, with the lawns sloping steeply to the sidewalk or merely lapping its edge like a green pond. Considering that America has the reputation in Britain of being an unruly and law mocking country, everyone seems to walk on the places provided for that purpose and I heard of no trouble with trespassers or flower pickers. Perhaps if they tried walling their gardens they might invite trespassers and flower pickers. As things are, the garden is there to be walked on, trampled on and even deflowered, so no one bothers.

Of the notorious lawlessness of America I met no more than may be observed in Britain. As far as trespassing on private property, I seemed to think that Americans were singularly law-abiding in this respect and in obedience to street and traffic laws. There are always people who prefer to run rather than wait for a green light, but the orderliness with which knots of people waited at the street corners and made few attempts to cross the street in the middle of the block was quite admirable.

The most striking reference to lawlessness was an unintentional piece of satire I observed in a western city. There was a large and florid building in the centre of a green plot near the centre of the city. "Justitiae Dedicata" was imposingly inscribed above the door. Immediately beneath this was a small and frank announcement, "For Sale."

Referring back to the lawlessness of young people, an educational institution in an eastern city, which shall be as nameless as the western city quoted above, installed an arrangement by which, if the door leading to either the men's dormitories by way of the entrance hall or to the women's dormitories by the same way were opened after a certain hour, all the firebells rang with violence. The students were not told of this installation. One early morning an innocent girl went out to mail a letter, and instead of using the side door past the night porteress she crept through the other into the lobby, so as to go out by the centre door. To her horror, the firebells rang and dozens of people appeared, very alarmed, only to find an embarrassed young woman with a coat over her pyjamas holding a stamped letter in her hand.

I met very little rudeness in America and comparatively little inefficiency, but rather more than I expected with my exaggerated British ideas of American efficiency. The rudeness and inefficiency were generally associated and I met little of that charm and imbecility that can be so disarming and yet so exasperating in some of our continental countries. Post Office officials I found very reasonable except the one I had most to do with and he was about as unpleasant as anyone I have ever met. New York theatre box office attendants are reputed to be the rudest people in America, but I was fortunate, and I attended some thirty of New York's theatres and concert halls and totalled more than fifty performances, getting my own tickets in almost every instance.

The lapse in American efficiency and courtesy that impressed me the most took place in Hollywood. I bought a ticket to the Hollywood Bowl at a well known ticket office in Los Angeles. The concert was timed on the ticket to begin at 5.15 p.m. I went, and saw several other people arriving just around five o'clock. There were no crowds, however. Upon inquiry at the ticket office at the Bowl I was told that the concert began at 8.15 p.m. Why, then, I demanded, was 5.15 stamped plainly on my ticket? That was an error, the man in the office said. But why, I asked, hadn't the man who sold me the ticket told me so when I bought it?

He was sorry, he admitted, and would be glad to take the ticket back and give me my money for it. For some reason this suggestion that I was fussing over a few dollars infuriated me.

"I don't want the money back," I explained, "and as it happens I am free to come to the concert this evening, but I think it unreasonable to be dragged out to Hollywood three hours too soon when I could have been doing something else."

He was sorry, he repeated.

"Couldn't you stamp the altered time on the ticket with a rubber stamp?" I asked, thinking benignly of posterity killing three hours in Hollywood when it would rather be doing something else.

"No," he growled and went to answer the telephone.

Soothed ultimately by the concert, which was fairly good, I recollected that the unfortunate man at the Bowl had had to explain the whole thing to dozens of irate people before I arrived on the scene with my bright ideas about rubber stamps, so in my large-hearted way, I forgave him, though I doubt if that is any comfort to him now.

Once, in New Mexico, in spite of the heat and my long and weary search for a jack, I found inefficiency amusing. It was in a tiny place called San José. I had walked some distance in the blazing sun to find the only garage deserted. I inquired of an old man in the village where the owner might be. When finally he understood what I wanted, for he was not only Spanish but deaf, he pointed over the desert.

"You see that house," he said.

"Yes."

There was indeed, a house, perched on a gentle slope.

"You see that man on the roof?"

"Yes."

"Well, he's the guy that owns this garage."

Feeling that the genuine old Spanish life was not yet gone from the great South-West, I walked to the house and shouted to the man on the roof. Fortunately, he was neither Spanish nor deaf.

Main Street at its worst is still to be found anywhere from Kennebunkport to San Diego and from Seattle to Miami. There is the standardization, the cheapness, the sentimentality, the pie and ice cream, the blaring radio, life as plodding and dull as in the suburbs of large cities, the eternal small town with its small ideas and small ambitions. There is the Fried-Klam-Kozy-Kamp-Kumfy-Kottage America. There you find the roadsides sprinkled with notices that do their pitiful best—A friendly city—A home away from home—Didn't you like Keene?—You'll find friends in Jonesville—The Biggest little city in Wyoming—You'll like Hot Springs—Glad you came—Come again—Everybody welcome —A Good Place to Eat—Good eats—Drive carefully, we love our children—Watch Nunn grow.

New England and the South would like to think that the Middle West is the home of Main Street and that dreary ooze of mass mentality that dishes up sentimental telegraph messages for Mother's Day, for the arrival of a new baby, for a wedding, for a birthday, for a christening and for Saint Valentine's Day.

To do the Middle West justice, the cheap vulgarity and the craving for a pathetic elegance typical of mass mentality are to be found all over the United States and, as we know quite well, over Britain too.

In America it takes the form of standardized witticism, a leaning towards quaintness and a love of euphemism. A restaurant will hang on its walls "Mary had a little lamb—What will you have?" and the joke will hang there for ten years or more until the very mention of Mary or lamb puts you in a state of depression that even beef and looking out of the window fail to dissipate.

The idea that a joke, however uproarious it may be at first sight, palls on frequent repetition, does not seem to have struck them. There will always be some people, they hope, to whom even the Mary and the lamb joke is new, and beside the happy tinkle of their surprised laughter what is the savage irritation of the thousands who have seen the thing forty times?

One effort at cheer in a western village ran this way:

> "We'll crank your car,
> We'll hold your baby,
> We make good coffee
> And we don't mean maybe."

As it was, my car needed no cranking, I had no baby, and their coffee was foul.

The mania for quaintness can be seen anywhere in the single word "shop." The word itself, being more English than the ordinary American "store," its use is an affectation. But the simple affectation is not sufficient. We must not only be quaint. We must be mediaeval and have "shoppes."

"Men's shoppe" is considered effeminate, but sometimes occurs. Occasionally one side of a hotel lobby will show "Beauty Shoppe," all feminine and Plantagenet, and opposite will stand "Men's Shop" in its bare virility.

The simple "shop" and quaint "shoppe," however, are falling into disfavour. The more original owners of the beauty establishments in particular, are now vieing with each other in advertising Beauty Box, Beauty Bower, Beauty Parlor, Beauty Salon, Beauty Booth, Beauty Nook, Beauty Studio, Beauty College, School of Cosmetology, Beauty Service, Beauty School, Shop of Beauty, Salon de Beauté and, their most triumphant—Nook de Beauté.

In New England, to which I am very partial, I was horrified to see, near one of its loveliest villages, a notice advertising "Ye Olde Gasse Statyone."

I am still wondering whether that is a genuine example or a delightful satire.

In ordinary parlance the terms cuspidor, thermidor, humidor and servidor make you feel as if your tongue was wearing a kid glove, and in California there was a butcher's shop which called itself a "meat studio." It is no longer there, but there may be others.

On the analogy of cafeteria I have seen Groceteria, Shoeteria and Grabeteria, this last being a curious mixture of straightforward vulgarity and elegance. The shop which calls itself the "Pay n' take it" harks back to the standardised witticism. I saw no laughing, happy faces walking in under the sign. They were all very tired of that one.

A "pantorium" seemed an unnecessary term for a shop that sold pants, or as we British say, with our own touch of elegance, trousers.

On one of the finest streets in New York City I saw an establishment which advertised itself as practising "Dehairolysis." That impressed me as being the strangest effort at learned elegance I met in three years.

All this goes hand in hand with a general

N—a

lack of culture, and if I use the Middle West as an example, let it not be thought that I blame or despise this great area in the centre of North America. But what are you to expect of a small town a thousand miles away from the coast that not long ago was a gas station on a highway and nothing more? How can the people who collect around a gas station and form a community there know anything of Elena Gerhardt or Seurat?

There is a small city somewhere in the Middle West. It is about the size of Canterbury in Kent. It has a population of a little over twenty-five thousand people.

What do these twenty-five thousand people need most, or think they need most, going on the assumption that supply meets demand? If after this I am met by a midwesterner who wants to live in a town that has one restaurant but forty-eight nurses, let him move on from the one I am describing. It is quite definitely not his town at all.

First on the list come the automobile service stations, sixty of them. These are not intended exclusively for the use of the native twenty-five thousand, but also for natives of other communities at present not in them but engaged in travelling. However, we can assume that the natives of Kentville (we can call it that in honour of Canterbury) travel too, so it all works out evenly in the end.

After the sixty service stations come the forty-eight restaurants, followed rather unflatteringly by thirty-nine physicians and thirty-seven dentists.

The next batch gives us thirty-one schools, twenty-nine automobile companies, twenty-six garages, twenty-four beauty parlours and twenty drugstores.

Less in number, but very important, are the twelve radio equipment companies, twelve churches, ten hotels, ten women's apparel companies and ten billiard parlours.

Less in importance come seven movie theatres, six department stores, six refrigeration companies, five funeral directors, five taxicab companies, five ice-cream companies, five radio repair companies, four osteopathic physicians, four five and ten cent stores, three yeast companies and two travel bureaux.

There is one bookstore, one nurse, one bowling alley, one window cleaner, and one potato chip company. And that is Kentville for you.

When the population is not working or sleeping or reproducing, it apparently drives in cars, eats, beautifies itself, is ill, consults the dentist, tinkers with the radio, goes to church, dresses as stylishly as it can afford, plays billiards, goes to the movies, shops and occasionally leaves Kentville. It reads little, sometimes eats a potato chip, and dies.

Substitute golf and tennis for billiards, reduce the automobiles and the ice cream and you have middle-class England.

Like middle-class England the fiction read in middle-class America is of the amorphous, fairly grammatical kind except that the American tendency to run to extremes is illustrated in the preoccupation with sex in its cheaper and more sordid aspects.

In a California hotel situated in an inland town of no distinction I came across a library list of some hundred books. The titles were so obviously of a kind intended to attract the cheap reader that I thought it worth while to jot down about a third of them.

Here they are: "To-night or Never," "Expensive Women," "Lady with a Past," "Boy Crazy," "Wife by the Hour," "Strictly Dishonorable," "Guilty Lips," "Street of Women," "Week End Wife," "Kept Woman," "Pavement Lady," "Second Hand Wife," "The Chastity of Gloria Boyd," "Only Human," "Youth Cries Out," "For Hire," "Forever Engaged," "Young and Healthy," "For Men Only," "Virtue O.K.'d," "Untarnished," "Bought," "Impatient Virgin," "Twilight Men," "Week End Marriage," "Broadway Virgin," "Constant Sinner," "Free Lady," "Way of Some Flesh," "Ladies of the Evening." And of course, "Lady Chatterly's Lover" and "The Well of Loneliness."

And yet you meet people who want to read, to listen to music, to understand art. The larger the city, naturally, the more people aiming at culture you will find.

In a bookstore in Minneapolis a salesgirl told me that people bought plays to read in large quantities in the twin cities. The inhabitants, she said, wanted culture and wanted drama, but they had only three or four good plays a year actually performed in the cities, so they read the New York papers and demanded copies of the New York theatrical successes. They had a stock company, but it was very poorly run, and they had so often seen performances that made tolerable good plays seem dull that they now fought shy of all companies unless well known actors were playing. When the Lunts came to Minneapolis the theatre was booked weeks ahead. The salesgirl attributed this severity and caution to the Scandinavian temperament. Rather than encourage mediocrity they apparently tend to suppress what small talent there may be among local theatre groups. There is much to be said on both sides. It is hard on the struggling youngster, but better in the long run to create and maintain high standards.

In other cities there are bookstores and colleges and concert halls and little theatres, and most university towns are very satisfactory places in which to live.

The general attitude towards college is different in America. A college education, like a refrigerator, is a necessity, not a luxury. You can work your way through college, either by waiting at table or doing office work for a certain number of hours a day during term time or by working at a full time job during vacations.

Young Americans are very persistent and resourceful if they determine to go to college and their parents cannot afford to pay their fees. They will sell magazines from door to door, they will become waiters in restaurants, they will work as ice men or rangers and almost anything you can think of. In any university town café the waiter who serves you might be researching for his Ph.D.

In America it is easier to earn money in spare time, and the general lack of permanence helps. Employers in England always seem to imagine that you intend spending your whole life doing the job you are applying for. Not so in America. There is, of course, the white collar class, but quite penurious people flitting from job to job scorn them as slaves. Salaries are higher, of course, and though the cost of living is higher, there is greater elasticity. You can earn a fair amount just doing odd jobs, and you can live cheaply if you share an apartment and eat at inexpensive cafés. Americans of good family are not as fussy as English people. Men and women accustomed to luxurious living at home will take a tiny room and eat sitting in rows on little stools in a drugstore if they want to go through a college year on eight hundred dollars instead of three thousand.

If you visit any schools or colleges in America you should see a football game in the late Fall, an ice hockey game in the winter and a baseball game in the summer. You should attend a preliminary pep meeting before a football game. If you get to understand American football you can enjoy a big game between any of the great eastern teams, Yale, Army, Harvard, Navy and Princeton. It is a spectacle as well as a game. A Saturday morning in the football season has an atmosphere all its own if you are in one of the university towns of the East. The campus is full of admiring aunts and mothers, and there are many girl friends about. Small boys sell coloured feathers for display and all sorts of emblems with the letters of the opposing teams on them. Everyone is excited, and the streets are full of cars all trying to park themselves and being moved on by the town police. Restaurants serve slightly larger meals and double their prices.

The game itself always seems an anticlimax after the morning's tension, unless it happens to be an exceptionally good game. It is all rather like Boat Race Day in London, except that it happens every Saturday, the crowd and restlessness increasing in proportion to the importance of the game.

By the early evening the aunts and mothers are packed off home but the young women stay around, and very many of them become very intoxicated. Game nights are usually lively.

You have probably seen ice hockey in England. It is one of the most exciting and beautiful games of any to watch. If cricket bores you, you will like baseball, unless all games bore you. If you are a cricket enthusiast, you will doubtless dislike baseball.

Young Americans are usually good swimmers. The habit of spending the entire summer vacation on lakes in the northern states has given them the opportunity almost to live in the water from June until September from an early age, so that by the time they reach college age they are very skilful indeed.

The European, criticizing the American, often ridicules his statistical mind and his passion for size and quantity. This part of the American's nature is linked up with his youthful attitude, his eagerness for learning and discovery, and his readiness to marvel as contrasted with the average Englishman's self-conscious and blasé maturity. The young American, whether an undergraduate or a business man of sixty, is never ashamed to breathe "Gosh!" and just gaze at something which surprises and moves him. The Englishman, particularly the southern Englishman of university education, refuses to be caught off his guard, and will conceal his natural emotion of admiration or wonder and even disparage what he is really moved by lest he should open himself to ridicule for his *naïveté*.

Megalomania, where it occurs, is a distressing symptom. I knew of a child who ceased to be interested in the *Berengaria* on which his parents were sailing to Europe and refused to see them off because his father told him it was not the biggest ship in the world. The boy was seven and passionately fond of elephants, but of no other animal.

Many people show a tendency to admire only the biggest things, the highest peak, the widest river or the tallest building, and will travel miles to see the Grand Canyon, the Niagara Falls or Pike's Peak, and ignore as beautiful smaller canyons and falls and mountains.

This is linked up with a certain lack of individuality in sight-seeing. The American

tourist in Europe has already been ridiculed
enough. On his behalf it might be said that
when he has saved up enough to come to
Europe, the amazing variety of small countries
with completely different languages and
customs proves too much for his curiosity and
enthusiasm. His own country does not differ
as much in three thousand miles as Europe
differs in three hundred. He wants his money's
worth. After all, Europe is three thousand
miles away for the easterner and five thousand
or more for the westerner, and it may be some
time before he has such another opportunity.
Who can blame him for not bothering to "soak"
in the atmosphere?

This defence of genuine curiosity and enthusiasm, however, does not cover the mass
level of intelligence that seems to hang like an
albatross about the necks of most Americans
who travel in groups.

I travelled on a boat from Los Angeles to
New York with a boatload of middle-class
Americans. The story is doubtless the story of
any cruise, with the community life taking
shape in the general detachment of being at
sea, the friendships, the hatreds and the
scandals.

There was a lady missionary on board. One
afternoon I sat at the same table at tea with
the lady missionary and a lady drunkard, each

being coldly polite to the other. One radiated, except at this tea, goodwill and sang contralto songs and the other was always to be seen making her way unsteadily to the bar or more unsteadily from it.

There was a pink and white woman from New York, who, I was told, had gone to California to marry a gentleman there, but when she discovered that he operated a fruit selling stand, she took the first boat back to New York. There was the boy athlete of advanced years, the man chaser with steady eyes and a veil, and two steady drunks. It was rumoured that the pink and white lady was ordered out of the boy athlete's stateroom by the boy athlete's wife and that later, the pink and white lady, while in her cups, discovered the veil and the steady eyes at their business and shouted, "So this is what you call good, clean fun?"

In addition to these leading players, there were minor actors—a New York Jew, several decaying gentlewomen, crowds of ardent bridge and poker players, a plump German and his Frau, visiting a daughter in Guatemala, a couple of Polynesians with an odious child whom they would never leave alone, a dope fiend, two hearty Iowans, amateur humorists, a journalist or two, an undergraduate, some wealthy business people, several married couples and several widows.

Most of the people seemed bewildered and a little frightened when they had a few hours on shore. They clung together in large groups and did the same things as everyone else without stopping to think whether they really wanted to do these things or not.

Soon after landing in the various tropical ports, they collected in the first American bar they could find, where they proceeded to do exactly what they had been doing some six or seven days on the boat—play the piano, dance, sing and drink.

Apart from the desire to be photographed in the tropical surroundings and a tendency to buy haphazard anything the natives offered for sale, there was very little real interest shown in the nature of the villages, the people or the life there.

One young man in Honduras was looking desperately for someone to photograph him with an ox. He saw me and begged that I should oblige him. He gave the owner a gratuity, waved him out of the picture and then stood, his arm resting lightly on the horns of the bored looking animal. I hope it was a good picture. My hand was shaking a little.

As we came back to the boat we were laden with packages. Many brought shoes and fruit and hats and pottery, and several brought bottles of rum. One admitted frankly that he just didn't know what he was going to do with all this junk, but that he just had to buy it when he saw it.

Towards the end of the twenty days people began making a tour of the entire boat with little notebooks, asking everyone to write names and addresses and clever little poems. Friendliness was rife on the last day, and everyone promised to write to everyone else. Whether they did so I do not know.

Altogether, this little reminiscence is not flattering to middle-class America.

I think it fair to state, however, that boats always bring out the worst in people. Besides, on land, you can always avoid those you dislike.

American parties are much the same as British ones and if you like parties you will have plenty of opportunity of indulging this pleasure, since Americans love to have English people at their parties. You have no sense of humour but you are very quaint and charming.

I went to two Hallowe'en parties in America and liked them. One of the two didn't allow us to duck for apples because of the possible infantile paralysis infection, a much dreaded disease in America.

Hallowe'en is made much of in America. Huge yellow pumpkins had been carved out with all sorts of queer faces, and hollowed in

the centre, so that candles shone vaguely
through the carvings and lighted up what was
left of the pulp and rind of the pumpkin. One
enormous pumpkin was a work of art. It had
all the letters of the alphabet neatly carved
on it, and should have been preserved and
exhibited with Victorian samplers of like
design.

There were three log fires, and apples hung
from all parts of the room. These were later
pulled down and hygienically eaten together
with little individual pumpkin pies. With
these we drank sweet cider. At midnight we
popped corn over the smouldering fires.

If you have never popped corn, you do it this
way.

You take the yellow grains and put them
into a wire basket on a handle, looking rather
like an old fashioned warming pan. Then
you hold the pan over the fire and shake
steadily. After a few minutes, the corn begins
to jump about. Each yellow grain bursts into
a white bulbous mass of delectable floury stuff.
When all the corn has popped, you empty it
into a bowl, sprinkle some salt on it, spread
butter into it and eat it with your fingers, a
sticky business.

Popcorn is much eaten at football games,
but you have to do without the butter there.
Men with little carts pop it and sell you bags

of it for five or ten cents. You can also get candied popcorn, and if you are the kind of person who puts sugar on porridge you will like it. Even if you don't offend the Scots with your treatment of porridge, you may still like candied popcorn.

Another fireside eating game regarded with some aversion and suspicion by some hidebound English people is the toasting of marshmallows. They must be good marshmallows, not the soapy, frothy kind that come in nauseating pinks and corpselike whites. They should have that firm, leathery look which every good marshmallow wears. You stick the marshmallow on the end of a fork and toast it gently over glowing coals. If you are careless, you burn the thing and it flops and melts into the fire or slips off the fork. If you are skilful you toast it evenly all over and it swells to double its normal size and is very delicious to eat. Marshmallow toasting is a feminine hobby, much practised in women's colleges all over the country.

A less evanescent and cloying joy is a steak roast. Get some Americans to take you on one.

On the subject of food, it might be good to attack on the basis of American accusations regarding the dullness of English food. Their chief complaints are that we just boil our vegetables and make no attempt to serve them interestingly, and that our coffee and ice-cream are very poor.

The Englishman is a little vague about the vegetables, indignant about the coffee, which he likes made with hot milk, still more indignant about American tea, and merely distant about ice-cream.

I was once discussing meat with a young man from Britain. I said I thought English meat rather better.

"Of course," he said, "everything is better in England."

"Oh, no," I protested, "ice-cream isn't!"

"I don't like ice-cream," he said, and the argument was closed.

It happens also that I dislike ice-cream, but there is no denying that American ice-cream is more appetizing than the sickly mess you are expected to eat in Britain.

Before we mention another article of food let us wrestle with the whole business of tea and coffee, and let us do it with cool heads and an eye to improving the general taste for these excellent beverages.

Tea is not difficult to obtain in America, and can generally be served at any meal in most restaurants, so that those Welsh and Irish people who like tea at other times than at four o'clock may have it. The tea is not as a rule good in America and is faultily prepared. In the summer, iced tea is a common beverage, and some waitresses express astonishment if in the summer you still want hot tea. Iced tea may be made with green or black tea, and is served with half a lime or with slices of lemon. Some people put cream into their iced coffee, but it is not usual to do this with iced tea.

When asking for hot tea in America, you had better stipulate black, unless you want green. Actually black is commoner in the East, but green is often served in the South and West.

If you like your tea of normal British strength, ask for double strength, that is, for two tea bags, for almost everywhere you go they will use tea-bags, and one is not enough.

If you take milk with your tea, ask for cream, and the same kind of thin cream that you get with your coffee will arrive in a small pitcher. If you prefer lemon, it will usually accompany the tea.

Most American restaurants do not heat the teapot before putting in the tea-leaves, and they seldom use freshly boiling water, and almost never do they put in enough tea. The tea is therefore weak and flat, and only the hot water part of it is refreshing.

The general method is to put only one tea-bag into the pot and pour hot water or stale boiling

water over it. The result is so weak that a
quarter of the tiny pitcher of milk will turn
it a pale buff colour. Sometimes a pot of just
hot water will arrive, or worse still, a cup of
hot water, with a dry tea-bag slung outside the
pot or reposing impotently in the saucer. You
then dip your tea-bag and watch the liquid
slowly darken. You may, if you like, drink
this concoction, but it is wiser not to. If your
tea-bag arrives dry, you have every right to
send it all back and tell them how to make it.
The deceitful wench who listens to you with
a nasty sneer on her lips will probably just
plunge the offending tea-bag into the now
frigidescent water, and bring you that.

I knew of an Andover boy who used to heat
a little pot of water in his room every afternoon.
As it boiled, he would remove the lid and dip
and re-dip a single tea-bag. How frequently or
for how long he dipped I do not know, but the
result was his afternoon tea.

I also heard of some Americans who, being
possessed of a tea-bag, heated some water, put
it into cups and dipped their tea-bag several
times, each into his cup. When one had dipped
he passed the heavy wet bag dangling on the
end of its string to the next, and so on. The
story sounds to me an invention by an Englishman, and I do not know how many Americans
were assembled at that tea-party. At all events,

one of them, when ridiculed for the tea-bag ritual, is alleged to have replied, "It's a good idea. You see, you can make the tea as strong as you like."

Canadians are much more British in their tea-drinking. In Montreal, forgetting that I was again in the Empire I asked a waitress for tea, and as she went I called as an afterthought, "With cream, please, not lemon." The Canadian girl gave me the kind of look that made the Empire what it is to-day, and said tartly, "We never serve tea with lemon here."

I suspect that this was a sweeping generalization, since I think tea with lemon can be obtained widely in Canada.

The best tea I ever had in America was at Montecito, California, even better than tea I had made myself from a tin procured at Fortnum and Mason's and treasured carefully. It was in a little house, apparently unadvertised, near the main road to Santa Barbara. A Scotswoman served us, and set out thin sandwiches, and many, many plates of delicious scones and cakes, among them jumbles. Thin sandwiches are unusual in America. If you are stupid enough to ask for sandwiches with your afternoon tea you will get a tremendous triangle with a wobbly upper deck and a slippery filling of lettuce and tomato or cream cheese and olives, or even peanut butter. In a city you may obtain thin slices of buttered toast with jam or marmalade, or just cinnamon toast, but as a rule there is a lack of delicacy about what is offered at teatime, except in private houses and not always there. A small restaurant will give you a huge hunk of layer cake or angel cake or pound cake, and in a village, they will offer you pie instead of cake.

As for coffee, the faults in the British making of coffee are much the same as the American faults in making tea. It is a little risky to generalize on questions of personal taste, but if the English are right when they say that the Americans have obviously not cultivated a taste for tea if they can drink the insipid brew that they usually get there, then the Americans are right when they complain that British coffee is never strong enough, and that hot milk is a mistake.

There are several methods of making coffee, and the simplest is probably the best. Use a heated pot or covered jug, as in the making of tea, and let the water be boiling. Let the coffee draw in a hot place, but do not boil or stew it. Strain it or don't strain it, as you please, and serve black, pouring into a cupful a small quantity of thin cream (not half clotted), about as much as you would use for tea. Use pure coffee, not a blend of coffee and chicory, and measure almost a flat tablespoonful of coffee for every cup required, or a heaped dessertspoonful, no less.

Only one person out of ten will agree with the above directions, since coffee making is a personal art, but it will at least be a definite break from the average British coffee and it satisfies a convert to American coffee making.

The kind of coffee described is the kind that you drink fresh, not the next day or the day after.

If you are ever taunted on the subject of British coffee by an American, find out tactfully from what part of the States he comes. If he is not a southerner, assume a fine scorn and tell him that only in Alabama, Louisiana and Mississippi can really good coffee be obtained. All southerners, except those that hie from other states than the three mentioned, will support you in this and agree that the coffee, and most other things if you let them, are inferior north of the Mason Dixon line. Actually I found New Orleans coffee rather a fearsome brew, but that was doubtless due to my inexperience. Two years later, a girl from Mississippi made me some coffee, which she alleged to be the real southern coffee, and it was excellent, very strong and rich, but not in the least bitter. However, even if you don't like southern coffee, you can use it as a weapon if you ever have any trouble with northerners.

As for vegetables we had better just admit

that our cooking of them is a little dull and that our choice is limited.

In addition to the usual boiled, baked and mashed potatoes we might eat them creamed or French Fried or Lyonnaise. The French Fried potatoes must be good, however. Even in America I have often had long dry uninteresting things that are certainly not French, can hardly be called fried, and I sometimes doubted whether they could honestly be called potatoes.

Sweet potatoes and yams are an acquired taste. I acquired a taste for them the first time they were served to me, but many British people dislike them.

Creamed carrots and peas, creamed celery and creamed asparagus would occasionally liven up an English meal. Beans, cauliflower, brussels sprouts, spinach, cabbage, parsnips, turnips and turnip tops we already know, but we seldom serve beets as a hot vegetable. Corn could be eaten more in Britain, either off the cob or stewed. Even canned corn, well cooked, can be very good. Corn and lima beans together make an interesting vegetable called succotash, and you can do things with a cabbage and turn it into cold slaw (often spelt cole slaw) if you like cabbage. Baked squash is good, and you may find that you like egg plant and mush, which is made of corn meal.

Any American cook book will give you all

you need to know on the preparation of vegetables.

Americans are good at beginning a meal with fruit juice or sea food cocktails and especially good at salads to eat after the roast.

Fruit juice cocktails may be made with oranges, tomatoes, grapes, apples, rhubarb, prunes, grape fruit, mint and cranberries, to mention only a few. Sauerkraut juice I could not manage to swallow, but you might.

I ate any kind of seafood with relish—lobster, crabmeat, shrimp, clam, and oyster—and if you like seafood, a term with which you will quickly become familiar, you will be happy on the American coast.

There are special seafood restaurants all along the New England coast and many in New York City. In addition to the cocktails, which you can have in any restaurant, these special restaurants serve broiled clams, fried clams, clam chowder made according to the recipes of Boston, Rhode Island, Long Island or Manhattan, oysters on the half-shell, oyster pie, oyster patties, oyster stew, clam broth, bluefish, whitefish, swordfish, other kinds of fish, lobsters, crawfish (known in England as crayfish), crabs, shrimps, fried scallops (called scollops) and almost anything that comes out of the ocean.

The Americans are inordinately fond of

game, and you will find turkey on ordinary restaurant menus all the year round and not only at Christmas and Thanksgiving. The turkey is usually called Vermont turkey, just as the duck is always Long Island duckling. You should eat fried chicken à la Maryland and squabs while you are in America.

New York restaurants are not representative of American food, and the foreign influence is strong. Some foreign dishes, however, are as American now as they are European, among them goulash, wiener schnitzel, pig's knuckle, ravioli, zabaglione and frog legs.

Americans, being accustomed to hot summers and warm rooms in winter, do not eat suet puddings and the stodgy, heavily caloried food that Londoners find so comforting on a dreary winter's day. They have lighter desserts (sweets), the heaviest being pies, blueberry, cherry, apple, pumpkin, raisin or lemon meringue, and if you garnish a pie with ice cream, it is "pie à la mode." Other desserts will be creamy and spongy or just the ubiquitous ice-cream.

They specialize in lunches suitable for a hot day, fork lunches that you can eat standing up, if you can find some spot to park your drink.

Try these one day:

Tomato juice cocktail. Smoked salmon sandwich and cold beer. Half a cantaloupe

stuffed with fruit salad ; or grape-fruit juice.
Strips of bacon with creamed mushrooms and
a salad on the same plate, the salad being
made of orange, pineapple and cherries,
dabbed with dressing and sitting on a lettuce
leaf. This followed with ice-cream, if you
like it, or if not, banana cream cake and coffee.

You will already have observed the American
habit of eating with the fork in the right hand
and laying down the knife before every mouth-
ful. You will also have become accustomed
to the six o'clock dinner.

It is well known that Americans hurry over
their food, and that they have developed the
soda-fountain habit as far as it will go.

It is true, I think, to say that the Americans
have a higher standard of food but a lower
standard of surroundings, or perhaps a greater
elasticity in their standards of surroundings.
Quite wealthy young people will sit on stools
and eat in depressing little drugstores, and not
only once in a while, but regularly. What is
more surprising is that the gloomiest little
cafés can produce a dollar dinner for you at
a moment's notice. Country cafés and small
inns in England run to little more than cold
ham and tomatoes or fried eggs and bacon. In
America some of the most unpromising little
places will produce soup, turkey, three vegetables, pie, ice-cream and coffee, and when

you are hungry and would even welcome cold
ham as served in rural England and Wales,
you will not think a dollar excessive for a
really good meal.

Americans very dutifully eat their cereals at
breakfast. They also drink their fruit-juice or
eat various kinds of melon—musk melon,
honeydew melon, cantaloupe, water-melon or
papaya, and grape-fruit, grapes, apples,
peaches, pears, apricots or sliced oranges.

With their meals they eat an interesting
assortment of breads. Instead of the stony
roll or the uncompromising slab of white bread,
there are poppy seed rolls, caraway rolls, corn
muffins—muffins not being muffins in the
British sense of the word, but little scones—
corn bread (like the kind you eat in the West
of Ireland), raisin bread (like Welsh bara brith),
and southern hot biscuits and hominy grits,
biscuits meaning scones, not crackers.

This variety lends colour to the most ordinary
lamb chop and it would be good if the British
restaurant were to make their breads more
interesting.

Prohibition, and through prohibition, the
soda-fountain habit, have made Americans
steady drinkers of milk shakes and sodas, and
eaters of sundaes and sweet things of all kinds.

Even now, after repeal, though near beer
and root beer and patent drinks of all kinds

are not so widely consumed as formerly, soft drinks have not disappeared out of American domestic or public life, especially in summer, when anything cold and wet is pleasant.

Americans drink more cold milk and butter-milk than the British, and more water. When-ever you enter a restaurant the waitress will bring you a paper napkin and a glass of ice-water before she asks for your order. It is the usual welcome. During your meal, your glass of ice-water will be replenished from time to time. Many hotels advertise ice-water in every room. Office buildings and trains have water coolers in the passage ways. They are large glass affairs and you take a hygienic paper cup and help yourself to cold water out of a tap. And Central Heating being what it is, your thirst is not confined to the summer.

Alcoholic drinks have been improving steadily since repeal. Many young people who belong rather self-consciously to the cocktail age seem to imagine that our fathers and mothers knew nothing of Martinis and Manhattans. Recipes for them, however, together with recipes for gin rickey and sloe gin, are mentioned in the 1906 edition of "Mrs. Beeton's Household Management" without which no Edwardian household was complete.

Mint juleps are not as well known in Britain as they might be. Duels can be fought in the

South over the making of a mint julep and there is much argument as to whether you should or should not bruise the mint. Roughly, the idea is this. You pack alternate layers of shaved ice and fresh sprigs of mint to fill a tall glass. Upon this you pour the best Scotch or American rye whisky you can lay your hands on, together with a little sweetened water, and put the lot away in a refrigerator for an hour. Then you garnish with a sprig of mint and drink through a straw as the ice melts into the minted whisky. The best mint juleps are made in Kentucky according to Louisvillians, in Virginia according to Richmonders, and the Canal Zone according to the Hotel Internationale in Panama City.

The names of inns in Britain may be strange, but they can hardly be stranger than some of the names the ordinary American eating places adopt.

Here are some of them: Daisy's Food Shoppe, Billy's Lunch, Smith's Eat Shop, Bob's Café, Dad's Coffee Shop, Minnehaha Chicken Tavern, Copper Kettle Inn, Hiawatha Lunch Room, Green Lantern Grill, Spanish Village Tea Room, Oasis Dining Room, Nokomis Cafeteria, Rainbow Nite Club, Ideal Sandwich Shop, Grand Bar, College Smoke Shop, Log Cabin Chicken Shack, John's Place, New Deal Barbecue (or Bar B Q), New Style Chili Shop,

Commerce Dinner Shop, Tip Top Candy Shop, Stiffy's Lot, Candleglow, Taste Rite, Tick Tock, Mother's Cupboard, Hasty Tasty, Bright Corner, Do Drop In, Dew Drop Inn, Due Drop Inn. Strange names are not confined to the buildings but occasionally bestowed upon articles of food. One Eastern restaurant advertised a dish called "Chicken à la King en Pattie Shell," which gives you the feeling of a backwards and forwards motion across the English Channel.

In a Western hotel I saw an item on a menu that must have brought joy to the heart of any philologist that saw it. It was "Antlers T Bone Shoe Strings." Just that. And it cost seventy-five cents. It would be a pity to explain it, but what you get if you order it is a steak and potatoes. And you won't find it just anywhere.

Now that you can see an American joke, understand football, sit in a temperature of seventy-five degrees and make tolerable coffee, you should be able to join in with a crowd of Americans singing American songs. If you know the traditional English popular songs, the well-known Irish sentimental songs and a few negro spirituals, you will be well on the way to familiarity with their entire repertory. They are never tired of singing "Daisy, Daisy," the "Derry Air," "Believe me if all those endearing young charms," "My wild Irish rose," and "When Irish eyes are smiling."

Among negro spirituals the favourite is "Swing low, sweet chariot." "Swanee River" and "Old Black Joe" are well known in Britain, though the second is usually called "Poor old Joe" over here.

You should know the New York song which has had political significance in its time, and which is to America what "Valentine" is to France. It has a rollicking tune resembling "Daisy, Daisy." Its words are as follows:

"East Side, West Side, all around the town
　The kids sang 'ring a rosie,' London Bridge
　　is falling down.
Boys and girls together, me and Mami
　O'Rourke
Tripped the light fantastic on the sidewalks
　of New York."

"Frankie and Johnnie" you must already know. If you are not raised in the tradition of its thirty or more verses, you cannot hope to learn it now.

One southern song that you ought to learn is "She'll be comin' round the mountain when she comes." It was once a spiritual but like the hymn "John Brown's body" it has taken on a whole collection of verses with a comic flavour. You can dance the Virginia Reel to

"She'll be comin' round the mountain" or you can just sing it.

Others you might become acquainted with are "Old grey bonnet," "Jingle bells," "Carry me back to old Virginny," "My old Kentucky home," "Old grey mare," "A hot time in the old town to-night," "La Golondrina," "Sweet Adeline," "In the good old summer time," "On a Sunday afternoon," and "Aloha Oe."

Some college songs are known all over the country, but I met no one who had ever heard of the one so famous in England about the student in the Eastern train, with its reference to Bangor and the woods of Maine. Unless I just happened to meet people who did not know this song and never to meet people who did, this number apparently won popularity in England and was forgotten in America, like some originally American slang expressions.

The popular Christmas carol is "Silent night," Gruber's "Stille Nacht, heilige Nacht" without which an American Christmas is incomplete. It is known in England, but seldom sung outside doors with "Good King Wenceslas" and the other half-dozen.

Altogether, Americans sing more than the English, but rather less than the Welsh. Negro, German, Italian, Spanish and Irish influences have brought this to pass, and the Americans incline to spontaneous self expression more readily than the English. They are more quickly depressed, more easily overjoyed. Like the Celtic races, they behave in extremes.

Their faults are the faults of youth; reckless optimism, enthusiasm, vitality, sentimentality, sensuality, mimicry and impatience of restraint are among their qualities. Criticism they welcome. They are naïvely honest, and will make easy-going attempts to dignify and stabilize their mercurial ways of living, but the result of trying to impose European maturity and English dignity on Americans is either the forced and self conscious majesty of the D.A.R. (Daughter of the American Revolution) or hypocrisy, and hypocrisy is so foreign to the straightforward American that he would rather admit his simplicity and have done with it. Anglophile pretentiousness exists, but it is heartily ridiculed.

Above all, the Americans enjoy life. It is in their own way, and in a variety of ways, that they enjoy it, but they look forward like happy children to what the next day will bring. In this youthfulness and freshness lies their greatest charm.

It is easy for the British to hold out their prejudices against the Americans when they meet a few casually in Britain or on the Continent. It is hard to resist them if you live among them and know them very well. Like wicked infants, they have a way with them.

Meet Main Street

In Chapter VI.

CHAPTER VI

THE Middle West is a much maligned and despised part of the United States. It is not despised economically and is, in point of fact, one of the world's greatest granaries. Socially, it is regarded as beyond the pale, with the exception of course of the city of Chicago, and by some less prejudiced easterners, the cities of Cleveland, Detroit and Minneapolis. As soon as Sinclair Lewis's "Main Street" appeared, those uncertain areas known as the East, the South and the West disclaimed any connection with the Gopher Prairie that purported to describe the average American small town in any of the forty-eight states, coloured only with a few local differences.

The Middle West has come to be regarded as the dullest and most hopeless part of the States. It is easy to see why. It is in an adolescent condition as compared with the sophisticated East, the mature old South and the still youthful Far West. Indians and covered wagons no longer roam over Iowa and the Dakotas, and the Rocky Mountains are five hundred miles away. Adventure and high spirits are out West. East are the cities and that vague thing called culture. And among the cornfields of the upper Mississippi valley, life is just in the awkward process of growing up and settling down and being very bashful about it.

There are fourteen Middle Western States, though some of the eastern ones will try to call themselves East and some of the southern ones South and some of the western ones West. They are North Dakota, South Dakota, Nebraska, Kansas, Oklahoma, Arkansas, Missouri, Iowa, Minnesota, Wisconsin, Illinois, Indiana, Michigan and Ohio.

Some of Texas is Middle West in character, but Texas likes to think of itself as South or as part of the great and romantic South-West.

New Yorkers and Philadelphians regard western New York State and western Pennsylvania as Middle West, and Virginians are apt to regard West Virginia as not of the South, but we can put that attitude down to personal prejudice and omit those states that have too close affinities with the East and the South to be really midwestern.

Geographically, the Middle West is the enormous rolling plain that covers the centre of the whole of North America between the Rockies and the Alleghenies, and stretching from the Gulf of Mexico northwards through Canada to the Arctic Circle. Once it was politically as large and undivided a territory, claimed by the French and called Louisiana, well over a million square miles of fertile land. Beyond the Rockies was Spanish territory and east of the Alleghenies were the British colonies. In 1803 the new United States bought these million square miles for something like three million pounds, but you cannot hope to buy a square mile of the Middle West for three pounds in these days, nor for three thousand.

Some of the fourteen states have vast and valuable forests, most of them are rich in minerals, all of them raise farm cattle, and all of them grow cereals, fruit and vegetables.

The cities are not only meat packing and exporting centres, but lumber mills, dairy centres and canners of fruit and vegetables.

This vast plain produces corn (maize), wheat, barley, oats, rye, flax, potatoes, sweet potatoes, hay, rice, sugar beets, peanuts, tobacco, beans, peas, tomatoes, cabbages, onions, apples, pears, plums, cherries, strawberries, raspberries, grapes, alfalfa, sweet corn, maple sugar, sorghum syrup (millet), nuts, hops, melons, hemp, cotton, horses, mules, dairy cattle, beef cattle, sheep, pigs, turkeys, chickens, ducks, coal, lead, zinc, aluminum (aluminium), manganese, natural gas, petroleum, iron, gypsum, clay, salt, limestone, sandstone, silver, copper, graphite, asbestos, potash, cobalt, nickel, tungsten, granite, pumice, mica and silica.

And among timbers, hemlock, white pine, Norway pine, maple, birch, larch, beech, cedar, cypress, basswood, elm, ash, cottonwood, spruce, balsam fir, walnut, oak, poplar, box elder, and willow.

And as if this were not enough, you can fish for trout, perch, bass and whitefish, to mention only four, in the numerous rivers and lakes.

The Middle West is to be much respected, and the forty-two-and-a-half million people that live in it, from the humblest cottonpicker in Arkansas to the wealthiest débutante in Chicago, are certainly not to be ignored.

And if you are tempted to think of this plain as merely uninteresting cornfield and prairie land, remember the millions of acres of forest and the lakes and rivers that abound, cool pleasant places in the summer where city dwellers camp and swim from June to September. One eightieth part of the Middle West is covered with water. Of an area of about 880 thousand square miles, eleven thousand square miles are water.

If you drive across the Middle West, you will

now know what to expect, roads that run straight as an arrow for a hundred miles or more, cornfield after cornfield, farms and cattlefields, vegetable plantations, forests, lakes, waste land, an occasional city, hundreds of small towns and villages, hundreds and thousands of automobile service stations, some railroads (over a hundred thousand miles of them, but you see only one at a time, and they are far apart), fresh air and sky. In winter there is the freezing prairie wind in the north, and in the summer blazing sunshine, violent thundershowers of hissing rain that steams on the blazing concrete of the road you are travelling and is soon over, leaving a refreshing coolness that lasts for an hour, when the sun comes into its own again until the next shower.

The prairie country is at its best in eastern South Dakota and Nebraska and is very beautiful indeed, especially under the typical blue sky flecked with white clouds. The rolling prairie land turns from yellow and green to blue as it fades to the horizon. Each farmhouse has its little copse of trees around it, and a windmill, not the four handed type, but the little wheel or propellor blade type. The barns are rust red and the houses usually white. The cattle are brown. Van Gogh would have loved to paint it. Sometimes the wheat chaff is piled into great heaps in a field and when the rain has fallen the yellow deepens to a rich gold.

There is a magnificent sense of space in this country. The wind pushes strongly and freshly across the plain, the grass waves, the cattle sniff, and the clouds puff gently and sedately in the upper air. You can breathe in Nebraska. You can also breath at sea, but here you are twelve hundred miles from the Pacific and as far from the Atlantic, and that is assuming that you are a crow.

In northern Nebraska, as you go west, the rich farm land dwindles into sand, the corn-fields are fewer, the farms less prosperous, and the countryside looks more like the drearier stretches of Texas.

I drove across Nebraska twice, once with a forester and once without him. He told me that Nebraska may be divided into four main areas of vegetation—the hardwood trees following the valleys of the rivers Platte and the North and Middle Loup, the prairie region across the east and south, rich and fertile and now a definite corn belt, the short grass region in the far west of the state, and the sandhill region in the north.

Here the whole country takes on the appearance of a desert of sand dunes covered with short grass and flowers of various kinds.

This desert was made by the wind and is neither glacial nor alluvial, but aeolian. Sometimes the wind, having built a dune, decides to unbuild it. A sandy hole appears and the wind gradually pokes and whirls and scrapes it into a deep wide bowl, and the foresters call it a "blow-out." The chief cause of blow-outs is fire or over-grazing. Once the plant life ceases to have a firm grip on the sand, the wind begins to use the loose sand as a trowel, and if the hole is exposed to the west, the result is a huge cavity.

The narrow sandy roads run perseveringly through this desert country. Sometimes, when the flowers and weeds grow close to the edges of the narrow lanes, it seems as if you are driving through a garden. There are just two deep tracks for the wheels of the car. Between these tracks is a strip of coarse grass. On each side the yellow Japanese sunflowers (if it is summer) lean over the path, and there are other yellow flowers, four-petalled ones, and purple flowers in the grass beyond, and a cactus-like plant called prickly pear. Sometimes you see a snake or a tortoise, and sometimes you see nothing for grasshoppers. As the fenders and wings of the car brush the bending weeds, the grasshoppers leap jauntily in through the windows, or from all sides if the car is an open one. Sometimes they leap out again, but more often they have to be cleared out at the end of a journey. Many meet their death against the sharp hot radiator grid, and a stop at a village occasionally provides a meal for half a dozen small birds who collect and help themselves.

Two pieces of useful advice for driving in Nebraska. Never try to turn your car in one of these sandy narrow lanes. Just go right on. Better you should reach the first village over the line in South Dakota, turn around there and arrive a few hours late than stick in loose Nebraska sand. If you are tempted to attempt a turn, remember the time you first drove in thick snow without chains. Well, it's like that. And in Nebraska, off the main roads, it's quite likely that no one will pass until towards the end of the week.

The second piece of advice. Attach a piece of wire netting over your radiator, and then you will not have to have your radiator cleaned right out after every trip. This applies to other states, of course, but you pick more grasshoppers out of your wire shield in Nebraska among the sandhills.

The sand of Nebraska is extremely fine, and when the rain falls, it soaks quickly into the soil below, so rain has to be heavy to be in any way effective. Underneath the sand is gravel, which men pump up for use on the roads. At Halsey, a village of about a hundred and thirty people, I had supper with two men who were engaged in this kind of work. One of them had never seen the sea and had only once or twice been out of the state of Nebraska. The other, a round faced man of Scandinavian colouring, had travelled farther afield. Everyone in Halsey seemed interested in the rest of the world but not dissatisfied with Halsey. The rosy faced woman in the post office asked for a written account of who we were and where we were going, so that she might put it in the village newspaper. I asked her whether she ever longed for a larger place than Halsey. She said no. All her friends and interests were in the district, a few square miles in the middle of the Nebraska sandhills, and she knew all the hundred and thirty people of Halsey and quite a number in other villages.

Strangely enough for America, there is no cinema nearer to Halsey than fifty-six miles, unless they have opened one recently. The children I saw playing in the village were actually amusing themselves. They were revolving each other on a cartwheel stuck on to a stake in a yard. Later, tired of revolving each other, they revolved a cat, but apart from giving it some un-asked for excitement, they did not treat it unkindly.

There is a forest station at Halsey, quite a

unique affair. By way of experiment, they are growing trees in the sandhill country— country in which there have been no forests for centuries, possibly never forests at all. The only naturally growing trees in the sandhill region are mostly green ash, and are clustered along the rivers, along the Middle Loup river at Halsey.

So scarce is wood fuel in this part of America that local men will work for nothing at all just to carry away the wood, which they are given free, a very happy agreement. As a rule, the getting rid of waste wood in thinning out is an expensive item. Here, wood is so scarce and expensive that there has to be a rule that no one may take away wood less than an inch in diameter. If this rule did not obtain, the workers would take away every needle and cone in the forest. Close to the forest station was a nursery where the young trees grew before being planted out on the hillside. I shudder to think what a severe forest fire would cost in Halsey.

Halsey is a fortunate little village. There is something of national importance within sight of the crossroads in the centre of it. It is the chosen village out of hundreds like it. It has an air of purpose and individuality about it which sets it apart.

Not so Bassett.

Bassett, Nebraska, is in the centre of the United States. It is not quite in the centre of Nebraska, being slightly east of the central line and very much to the north of the state, twenty-five miles or so south of the South Dakota state line. One of the transcontinental highways runs through, or rather, by, Bassett, and it has a railroad station on the Chicago and North Western line. It is therefore not completely in the wilderness and may be taken as typical of the ninety-nine places you happened not to choose to stay the night. It just chances that, owing to factors of speed, hunger, the state of the road, the grade of your car, the weather, the time of the year and the strength of your eyes, you turn aside at Bassett, Neb. for the night.

The town has between six and seven hundred inhabitants and one hotel. Apparently one is enough, since there was another, but it is now closed. On the drab windows of the disused building is scrawled "Jesus is Coming." And if He means to make as humble an entrance into the world as He did last time, by all means let Him come to Bassett, Neb.

The existing hotel has a lobby with a black and white check floor, an inquisitive manager-ess, plentiful and nauseating cuspidors, a long table across which at any time of the day or evening you can find the manageress's husband in a dirty grey shirt playing poker with a man in a panama hat or a yokel in a black hat, puffing at a pipe.

In the window are tins and pots of plants, and against one wall a bagatelle board. On another wall is a weighing machine, a map of Nebraska, several calendars and advertisements, and a telephone. The walls are a blotchy green.

The main street of Bassett is not paved. It is just trodden down sand. There are trees here and there, and a pathetic strip of grass between the sidewalk and the road in the residential section, which is all of Bassett except the block that is the shopping section. Here are the usual stores, but none of the electric signs and bright lights of the established Main Street. The railroad tracks are at one end of the village. A train puffs over them once in a while and a bell tolls a warning to anyone who might not know with dismaying certainty the exact time when trains arrive at Bassett.

There is one movie theatre but it will probably be closed and advertising a show for next week.

That is all, except six hundred and thirty-five people, according to the census of 1930. Since then, these six hundred and thirty-five people have doubtless succeeded in adding to that figure. Soon they will want to be paving the

road. Someone will open up the closed hotel,
there will be two movie theatres, and healthy
rivalry will improve the pictures, a new beauty
parlour, a five and ten cent store, a restaurant
or two, and Bassett will grow. Chicago once
had only six hundred and thirty-five people in
it, and look at it now. All the Bassetts of
America tell themselves this, and there are
many hundreds and thousands of them. Glance
out of the train by day or by night on any
American railroad and you will see Bassetts in
plenty, white Bassetts, brown Bassetts, yellow
Bassetts, large Bassetts, small Bassetts, growing
Bassetts, shrinking Bassetts, all grinding out
the metabolism of America's enormous and
mysterious interior.

Meanwhile, in Bassett, Neb., between six and
seven hundred people live, love, work, play
and die, and are unnoticed and unseen if you
happen to stop for the night at Newport, a few
miles east of it, or Long Pine, a few miles west.

And the moral of this is—whatever you get
when you are in America, you may be certain
that you are missing a great deal more.

Just to the north of the sandhills is a village
called Brewster. Brewster is a baby Bassett. In
1930 there were a hundred and two people
living in and around Brewster. I saw about
twenty of them. It was almost so shapeless as
to be termed an embryo Bassett rather than

a baby Bassett. Its buildings were two short rows of shacks placed widely apart so that the sandy patch of ground on which stood one dilapidated Ford car would one day be Main Street.   Apart from this bunch of stores, a scattering of houses, there was nothing but sand and sky. That was Brewster.

Such is life and land across the wide Missouri river, that wide and sandy stretch of water spanned with iron bridges through which you can see outlined in girders the essence of Nebraska, space and powdered sand, blue sky and slow reflective water.

The best way to see the Middle West is to travel across it in a leisurely way, and when you come to somewhere that attracts you, stay there.   These fourteen states are not show places, whatever the advertisements may say, boasting as they do a collection of state parks, "scenic" drives, lake resorts, universities, monuments, Indian mounds, birthplaces and battle sites. Unless you are a very easily persuaded person, these blandishments will leave you cold. Every state in the Union has these, and the spots marked out for their "scenic" beauty are for the most part no more attractive than miles of country through which you can drive any day without the embarrassment of having it pointed out to you and being told to admire it.

Some of the Middle Western states have

definite attractions however, not possessed by other states and tracts of country deservedly famous for a consistent standard of beauty. Arkansas and Missouri can claim the Ozarks (aux arcs), which are called mountains, but which are really a forested plateau with a height of 1,500 to 2,000 feet, Michigan and Minnesota are proud of their miles of lakes and woods, Michigan also having dunes and beaches along the coast of the great lake which bears its name. Moreover, the locks at Sault Sainte Marie boast the greatest traffic in the world, Panama and Suez not being in the running at all, though better known to most British people. And Detroit is no city to be overlooked.

Minnesota can justly be proud of Minneapolis and Duluth, and as for cities, Missouri can claim Saint Louis, and Illinois the second largest city in the States, Chicago.

Ohio has four great cities, and Cleveland is one of the pleasantest cities in the country. It has an excellent railroad station.

Oklahoma's distinction is the Panhandle ranch country which it shares with Texas. And South Dakota is redeemed for its miles of prairie by the Black Hills in the South West of the state and the Bad Lands close by.

As a rule, however, you will find that the most lovable qualities of the Middle West will strike you when you are least expecting to be favourably impressed. And if you stay in one place in this great country, provided that you choose your place well, you will find the country demanding your affection and admiration in a way that you would never have believed possible when you merely drove through it condescendingly as most easterners and foreigners do.

By all means do the regulation things if you want. Visit the stockyards in Chicago, learn to know that city as well as you know, or should know, New York; have yourself taken over a Minneapolis flour mill, ride among the Black Hills, motor to the Bad Lands, stay in the Ozarks, but don't let this be enough. Be fair to the Middle West. Scorn if you like the Bassetts and Brewsters, but stay in some quiet place, a ranch in Oklahoma, a farm in Ohio or Iowa, a lake cabin in Michigan or Minnesota. There, and there only, will you come to understand what the Middle West meant to the first settlers and what it now means to the most sensitive of the forty-two and a half million people who live there.

One late summer I stayed in a house in Ohio. It was a frame house and had a porch. From the roof of the porch hung a seat, swinging on chains. Most chairs in America swing or rock, and are very soothing. When conversation gets tiresome, you can just rock your chair gently or creak the chains of your swing seat and madden the person who bores you. Little green lawns surrounded each house and there were shady trees along the road. Even suburban and small town Ohio has its attractions if you don't have to live there. The pleasant swish of garden hoses in the cool of the evening, the fresh smell of the air, the rattling buzz of the katydids, all gave the green and clustered streets an air of peace.

One day I went to a farm and stayed there until evening. On the way we passed a village called Gomer. It was almost entirely Welsh and the tiny village of Llanbrynmair in North Wales seems to have helped to populate this section of Ohio. The Welsh village lies in an agricultural district and rests in a gently undulating countryside. The Welsh-American village has a Welsh chapel, but otherwise it looks much like any other American village with its white frame houses, all set in green lawns and shaded with trees just as in New England. Around the village, the flat Ohio country stretches rich with farms and corn-fields.

I spent almost the entire day sitting on the porch of the white farmhouse, swinging lazily on a seat that depended from the ceiling. The September sun shone warmly on me. The hens poked around the lawn and the pigs snuffled hoarsely beyond the low white fence. I remembered with a sense of guilt that one of the chickens had been killed on my arrival, but its companions did not seem to be unduly bereaved and certainly bore me no resentment. Out in the field the men were busy cutting corn.

I visited the city of Cleveland on two occasions. The first time I stayed with friends in one of its residential districts and the second time it happened to be our second night's stopping place on a drive from Connecticut to Michigan. The car was an ordinary Chevrolet sedan and four of us entered it together with baggage, two typewriters, two tennis racquets, several boxes of cakes and sandwiches, and a hat in a brown paper bag. It rained for about a third of the trip and once the hat blew out and was nearly run over, but we got from New London on the Connecticut coast to the northern tip of southern Michigan without damage of any kind, but with a good deal of gentle and persistent aching. We made three social calls on the way, or we should have taken less than three days and a half for a mere eight hundred miles.

The two girls sat in the back and had to endure the brunt of the bumps and the inconvenience of the baggage, and I account it a tribute to young American womanhood to state that they looked smart and nonchalant even when they disentangled themselves from tennis racquets and typewriters and crawled out to lunch and dinner.

The first night we stopped at a place called Troy, in Pennsylvania. We had gone south some miles out of our way and it was dark when we reached Troy. It was a dull little place, but we found a tourist home with accommodation for the four of us. The girls were placed in a room with only one door and that door opened into our room. In the morning we awoke to a gentle tapping. The girls were up and wanted to get out and wash, and would we tell them whether they might.

The next night we reached Cleveland, or rather a suburb of Cleveland and stayed a mile or two east of the city so that we might see it in the morning as we drove on. It was a question, of course, of staying on the fringe of the city, anyway, since we were going to Michigan on slender means.

To stay on the east side of the city was my arrangement. None of the three Americans with me had seen Cleveland, but I had waxed so eloquent on its beauties that they had come to regard the city as my home town. As we drove through it next morning I pointed out the magnificent railroad terminal and wondered whether I should be so good-natured if I were being shown York Minster by an American.

The Cleveland house was interesting. The rooms were enormous and the rates were very reasonable. It was my turn to make inquiries and when I did so and told the couple who attended to me that we wanted two rooms, they consulted with each other and told me that they would have to hand over their own best room, with palatial bathroom attached. They didn't mind that in the least, they insisted, as long as they were quite sure that we were going to behave and not injure their very beautiful furniture. I assured them that the two girls were very well brought up and would injure nothing, and that even we men were safely to be trusted in a well furnished room. It was the lady of the house who seemed the more anxious to make sure who and what we were before she let us in. Her husband seemed unsuspicious from the first and whenever his wife disappeared he became apologetically friendly and confidential. It gave him great joy to ask us many questions and to recommend his special brand of safety razor blades, generously making us accept one each as a gift. He was a real-estate agent, he told us, and he had no children. It was easy to see that he wished he had, and it was sons, not daughters, that he wished. He was friendly towards the girls, but he became a father to us two men for that night and the following morning.

He heard us call each other by our first names, and before he had known us an hour he was using those names as if he had known us always. He spent as much time in our company as his wife would let him, and was delighted the next morning when we discovered a flat tyre and had to change a wheel before we drove off. He fussed around and helped and chatted and tucked the suitcases in the back, and as we drove away shouting "Good-bye" the plump little man with bright eyes was wearing a radiant and slightly sad expression. He was so young and playful in spirit and his wife was so hard and old. It seemed a pity that he had not three or four sons to whom he might recommend razor blades and in whose company he might tinker about with cars.

His house was a very pleasant one, and an excellent example of how fortunate you can be with tourist houses. Our room had a balcony. We could see nothing from it but masses of wet and blowing trees, but we could hear trains clanking along the railroad tracks below, and we knew that Lake Erie was beyond in a thick mist.

The following day we happened to drop in

on a college town celebrating its Graduation Day. Having friends in the town and college, we joined in the celebrations for two or three hours, and then sped westwards again.

In Michigan, where I stayed six weeks, there were miles of lakes and forests, a clump of garages, service stations, drugstores and sordid little restaurants on the main street and beyond —just sand.

The main diversions in this country are riding, boating and swimming, and at odd moments between meals, dropping into drugstores for sundaes or milk shakes or rich concoctions known as "velvets."

Swimming is a delight at any time of the day or night, once the summer has fully arrived. Until the middle of June the nights are quite cold, but the days are hot and sunny and dry. Occasionally, just before the weekly thunderstorm, the heat becomes oppressive, and you just have to wait until the huge clouds gather on the horizon and sweep slowly across the lake. Then, and then only, comes relief. The sunlight dies down and then goes out altogether, birds fly low over the water and there is a silence of expectation over everything. Then, a flash of lightning, one thunderous gust of wind and the pinewood roofs are echoing with the seething, leaping rain.

The next day, the sun will be shining again,

and the noon heat dry and fresh. The sky will be cloudless and the lake water, beautifully green and decorated with little white-capped waves, will plash seductively a few yards from the harebells that shiver in the grass. You are in for six or seven days of the perfect summer of the northern Middle West until the gathering heat and the exhalations of the lakes stage another storm.

The storms usually break in the evenings, from five o'clock until midnight, and if the lightning is flashing some distance away you can swim in the lake and let the lightning glow on your wet arms and outline the heavy rolling clouds on the horizon. If you dive and look up you can see the bodies of those with whom you are swimming like lumpy fish against the pale green of the lightning coloured water. If this curious under water entertainment pleases you, you can do similarly in moonlight or against the Northern Lights, which often give a magnificent display in the northern States and Canada.

A summer with Americans at a lake resort will invariably make you much more aquatic than you ever were before. In the Middle West, especially in Minnesota which has nearly four thousand square miles of inland water and a population largely Scandinavian, the standard of swimming in summer resorts is very high and an encouraging change from some of the clumsy splashing that goes on along most of the British beaches.

Minnesota in the summer is another good country to loaf in, to eat and sleep, bathe, boat and fish, sip tea in the afternoons, read and write, and think nothing of work and politics and finance.

I stayed for several days with a man who had a cottage on Mille Lacs. Mille Lacs, in spite of its name, is just a single lake, some twenty miles long and about thirteen broad.

In the cottage with us were my friend's father, who was a Judge in spring, Fall and winter, but a loafer in the summer, and the hired help, a handsome young Scandinavian girl who had wavy fair hair and blue eyes, and artfully wore a blue and white frock. The general result was more débutante than servant.

My general impression of Minnesota is of sunshine, water, the pleasant sizzling of breakfast on the stove, the Judge, going or coming from fishing, the morning breeze off Mille Lacs rustling through the trees, the Scandinavian whistling "Stormy Weather" in the kitchen or rocking on the porch to the rhythm of a radio foxtrot.

Breakfast usually consisted of bacon and eggs or sausages and potatoes, griddle cakes and maple syrup, and coffee. As we sat on the porch eating it, auriols and goldfinches would poke around the pump handle a yard or two beyond the screen door, and flickers, birds of the woodpecker family, sat against the trees and flitted busily around.

When it rained, there was noisy pouring on our wooden roof, a flutter on the surface of the lake, and quickly the woods became cool and scented, and the roads and brown wooden houses darkened. The rain never lasted long. One minute there were white waves in neat, evenly spaced little rows on the lake and the wind swaying the silver birches by the water, and the next there was a calm, and the sun came out from behind a cloud and grew warm, and soon everything was sunshine and tranquil gaiety again.

The Minnesota country, although flat and a thousand miles west of Vermont, is not unlike it in its lakes and woods. They grow maple trees, too, and collect the syrup, just like Vermonters. The breakfast syrup I had was from a local maple grove, and I met its owner. He was a man of a little over thirty and looked like a Scandinavian, but his father was born in County Tyrone.

One night we went to a dance at a place called The Green Lantern on Bay Lake, and we had with us two charming girls from Kansas, holiday makers in their own summer cottage.

The Judge was out fishing when we went, so we took a dilapidated little Ford, leaving behind the other car, a splendid creature with a radio inside and a speed of ninety.

We trundled the exquisite young Kansas ladies in the flivver and soon after we started dancing at The Green Lantern, the Judge drove up in *his* with the Scandinavian cook. It all made democracy seem quite delightful and very funny.

Riding in the bus on the main road to Minneapolis I noticed a number of Indian trading posts, a tent or two strung with basket work and popular tourist trifles, the midwestern equivalent of the British "Present from Brighton" and Goss china. Near one of them stood an uncomfortable looking Indian loaded with the complete insignia of his tribe, head feathers and all. The temperature was approaching a hundred in the shade, and the man was doubtless aching to tear off his trumpery which must surely have been winter garb, and slip into a fifty-nine cent shirt and a pair of duck trousers.

One of the most exciting things that ever happened to me overtook me between Sauk Center and Minneapolis, driving alone southeast across the prairie country of which Sinclair Lewis speaks so feelingly in his "Main Street." As it happens, Sauk Center was the author's birthplace and is said to be the original

"Gopher Prairie." And would you believe it
—they are proud of it. The place was honoured
by being chosen as the epitome of deadliness
and despairing lack of beauty, as typical of the
worst in American life. The first thing I saw
in its main street was a store window with
Gopher Prairie splashed across its windows.
That looked like shame! It was no more
prosaic or ugly than many small towns I had
already seen, and it was larger and more
prosperous looking than I had expected. But
there was no mistaking it. From the moment
the engine of my car stopped chugging I was
in the world that the book had painted for me,
and twenty years had made little essential
difference. Sauk Center was simply a larger
Bassett, Neb. Long Prairie, a tiny and lonely
settlement some few miles north of Sauk Center,
was a little Bassett, almost as embryonic as
Brewster, Neb, but rather more shapely. At
least, it had some shape in the summer, but I
dread to think what it must have been like in
winter with the prairie wind sweeping snow
unmercifully down the unprotected streets.

On the way across this desolate Minnesota
country I picked up a hitch hiker. He was a
farm lad, half Swede, half German, and he
stayed in the car for sixty miles or so. He
was pleasant and intelligent and he told me
that he pitied people who lived in cities. He

had recently been to the twin cities for a few days, but he preferred the farm country up near Brainerd. He himself worked in the fields all day, even when it was over a hundred degrees in the shade. He certainly looked it. His face was brick red beneath his tousled corn coloured hair. Often he went deer hunting in the forests of northern Minnesota or fished in one of its ten thousand lakes.

It was late afternoon as I left Sauk Center for Minneapolis. By this time I was alone again and the sky was grey and heavy. As I passed through the deadly little village settlements that are scattered along the road and railroad between Sauk Center and Saint Cloud, lightning flashed in the distance, and rain began to fall.

Just before sunset the prairie storm broke. The flashes ahead and on either side became more frequent, and vivid forks trembled to the ground in threes and fours. The road became wet and slippery so that I had to lower my speed by about ten miles an hour. Then a wonderful thing happened. I had noticed the reflection of a brilliant yellow western sky behind me as I drove east into the darkening grey cloud, but I was unprepared for the sudden appearance from behind a cloud just above the horizon of an amazingly intense, copper coloured sun. It came out in full and blazed frowningly on everything to the east. The dull gold cornfields suddenly glowed a rich red, the green clumps of trees about the farmhouses took on an unearthly burnished tint, the hay ricks shone like stacks of new coins, and ahead and on either side pale violet lightning flashed and flickered across and through and behind the leaden grey-black mass of cloud.

The fierce forks half scared me and half enchanted me with their brilliance. They quivered all around and criss-crossed against the sky, and the thunder rolled across the prairie with an empty roar that was nothing like the full-bodied crashing of mountain storms. Happy little paddocks hopped across the wet road, flapping moths swept across my headlights and an occasional gopher scuttled away into the grass at the side of the road.

A great wind rose from the prairie and buffeted the car. What with fearing to skid on the wet surface and fearing to be blown into a ditch my driving took on the tactics of a yacht at Cowes. The brilliance of reflected headlights made all a sudden blur, and then a lightning flash would turn the yellow and black uncertainty into a delicate lilac landscape, and then the darkness was more intense than ever.

The copper gold behind me in the west

gradually faded away, but before it went I saw a lake fringed with trees painted in the two colours, and two colours only, copper and slate, each ripple half copper, half slate, and a narrow strip of copper sky behind the slate-coloured trees and beneath the slate-coloured storm cloud.

In spite of my haste and hunger I stopped the car by the side of the road and looked at the breathlessly stupendous simplicity of that little colour scheme, until the light began to fade and the rain pattered more heavily and I thought friendlily and inartistically of mint juice cocktail, chicken and beets, banana nut cake and coffee. That was my dinner that evening, and welcome it was, too, after a long day's driving.

The next day in Wisconsin, driving to Madison and Chicago I was attacked by a less spectacular but considerably more alarming thunderstorm. This one, instead of being all around and very lovely to watch, was on top of me. I drove half in haste and half with great care to avoid skidding. I skidded once, but not dangerously. Every time I speeded up I seemed to be running right into the lightning, and every time I slackened speed, it seemed to be catching me up from behind. I began wondering whether or not the rubber tyres on a car were sufficiently safe insulation.

When my mind dwelt on insulation I was more or less at ease, but when I pondered on the steel and gasoline which I was trundling uncertainly over naked looking hills and beneath overhanging trees, I was not so happy.

I took refuge from the storm at Wisconsin Dells, in a little white frame house that was spotlessly clean and charged me just seventy-five cents for my room and bath. Wisconsin Dells seemed to be a resort, and upon inquiry I was told that many people spent the entire summer in this wooded region. I had my supper in a restaurant on Main Street. The street itself was full of puddles and the trees were arched and green in the lamplight and dripped rain heavily whenever the wind stirred. The air was sweet with the freshness of rain and the scent of wet timber in a lumber yard two blocks away. I saw very little of Wisconsin Dells, but next morning when I drove to Madison for lunch and arrived at Chicago in the afternoon, I realized what charming, unpretentious country it was in. Wisconsin is a little known state, and I made a note that if ever I had an opportunity I would get to know it better. The city of Madison with its university and its lake pleased me tremendously. I added it to Cleveland, Chicago, Detroit and Minneapolis as a Middle Western city of distinction and beauty.

R—a

A very good way of travelling across the Middle West in the heat of the summer is to avoid the land and take a boat over the Great Lakes. For a very moderate cost you can travel the length of lakes Erie, Ontario, Huron, Superior and Michigan in comfort. You can be cool when others are baking and you can go through the locks at Sault Sainte Marie, popularly called the Soo. You can reach Duluth, Minnesota, in the heart of the Middle West, from the Atlantic Ocean with hardly a break in your water journey, and you can see the Niagara Falls. If you start from the East you can also see the cities of Quebec and Montreal, the city strongholds of old French Canada, and the country between them which is as different from New England over the border as Sussex from Picardy.

The Canadian Middle West is not much different from the American, the same sky and space, the pure air, the corn, the flamboyant sunsets, the crashing storms, the heat in summer and the cold in winter, the prairie winds, the remote settlements and the dull little working towns.

This is Fort William on a sunny Monday morning in July. It is washing day. There are red brick houses and grey and yellow wooden houses clustered together beyond the railroad tracks. Each cramped little backyard is a-flutter with not very clean linen. The undergarments worn in Canada's Middle West seem much the same as those worn in Peckham and Wimbledon, and quite as unlovely.

There are ten or a dozen railway lines half covered with rust-coloured trucks, one line of which is slowly, oh, so slowly, moving. Between the rails, clumps of grass and weed grow. On the spire of the long landing stage shed sit nineteen seagulls. I know because I have just counted them. Most of them are silent and reflective, but occasionally one takes off and wheels around for a few minutes, returning presently to his place in the row and perhaps scaring off another to do the same. At all events there is a sad lack of originality in the proceedings.

A boy lazily rides a bicycle along an almost deserted street in the town, his white shirt reflected in a shop window as he passes.

The sun creeps higher and higher. If I took the trouble I suppose I could go into Fort William and find out exactly what happens there. I could interrogate the shopkeepers, visit the grain elevators, and ask to be shown a typical Fort William home and even eat a typical Fort William meal. At the moment, however, my desire is just to sit still and go on sitting still. That is how Fort William makes me feel. I shall never know anything about this town of twenty thousand people, and it would take much convincing argument to persuade me that I have missed a great deal. One day I shall hear a radio talk about the romance of wheat and feel sorry that I did not take an intelligent interest in this old Hudson Bay trading post. Until then I shall not have many regrets about Fort William. The river which runs into Lake Superior to the west of the town is called the Kaministiquia. That is something of which the other Fort William, under Ben Nevis, cannot boast, even if its chief industry is distilling.

The great bay outside Fort William is called Thunder Bay and the great rock in it called Sleeping Giant is said to be Hiawatha himself, sleeping there ever since that last evening when he pushed off his canoe and sailed into the sunset on the Shining Big Sea Water. If such is the case, somnolence overcame him very quickly after he started.

Port Arthur, Manchuria, looks very dull in pictures, but I am sure it cannot be as dull as Port Arthur, Ontario. It is four miles nearer the American border than Fort William, but that is very little comfort when you walk for two hours around its streets, for I was determined not to be unfair to Port Arthur, even if I did judge Fort William from a comfortable chair on the deck of a boat.

There is a Main Street parallel with the waterfront called Cumberland Street. On this street are one adequate looking hotel and two or three dingy ones. In one of the dingy ones was the usual office and a gloomy row of chairs facing the window. One customer, wearing a derby (bowler hat), sat in one of these chairs and stared disinterestedly into Cumberland Street. There were cuspidors in plenty to spit into, but he did not even spit. He just sat and stared. Therein lies the soul of Port Arthur.

Determined, however, to find something of interest in Western Ontario I looked about me. On a wall I saw an advertisement for cigarettes in the Finnish language. In the next block I saw a notice saying "Taxi Service—Billie Oikonen," and a few minutes later I was rewarded by hearing Finnish spoken on the street.

I took a glance at the telephone directory (philology becomes the liveliest thing in the middle of Canada) and noticed numbers of English and Scottish names, several Finnish names, a few Welsh and Irish names, and a smattering of German, Scandinavian, Italian and Slavic names.

The Public Library was on a street parallel with Cumberland Street. It had a shop window front, screened with netting and packed full of flowers and shrubs. I looked in at the door and caught a glimpse of a harassed looking library assistant and a long row of men and women reading or standing about.

I walked inland up the hill. From the coolness of the lake front it grew hotter and hotter. There were two or three churches and several quite large, prosperous looking houses on the hill overlooking the lake. Near the top of the hill was a disused tennis court. One net, torn to shreds, still sagged hopefully between a couple of rotting posts, and the white lines still indicated the boundaries, but the paving was in pieces, probably broken during the hard Canadian winter and not repaired in the spring.

The view from the ridge was a beautiful one—southward over Thunder Bay to Sleeping Giant lying on the low grey line of mist, and northward to rolling forest land. The air was warm and scented with pine. I walked towards the trees. The houses, once over the ridge and out of the coolness and beauty of the lakeward aspect, became small and poor, but some of them were quite pleasant and had little cottage gardens, blue with delphiniums. Life seemed happy enough in these little houses out of sight of town and water. A child in one of them was tinkling away at an imitation Mozart minuet. But when I walked down into the town again and saw the deadly streets and the two movie theatres, "Kongo" advertised at one, and "The Barbarian" at the other, I felt sad again and wondered how the unhappy people endured the winters, endured Port Arthur, and endured each other. Probably, as usual, I was wasting my sympathy.

I must confess that I was glad to pass under the iron bridge and enter Duluth, the gateway to Middle West America. But I would take that boat trip again any time.

I think I have been fair to the Middle West, almost indulgent in places. I admit hardly mentioning Chicago, after so much talk of New York. But Chicago is not typical of the Middle West. Nor is New York, I suppose, typical of the East. The truth is that, though I stayed in Chicago, I never knew it intimately. I was a stranger in Chicago, even in the pleasant University quarter where I stayed part of the time. I was at home in New York and in the Middle West.

You should be born in the South. If you just go there after growing up, you will never really know it. The South takes its time, and it takes your time if you are even to scratch the surface of an acquaintance with it. I wooed the South on four separate occasions and even now I do not know whether what responded was the South or just America below the Mason Dixon line. The two are not synonymous, though everyone speaks of them as if they are, and so shall I.

The South is famous for its hospitality, its cooking and its cotton.

Don't believe people who tell you that the South is unbearably hot in the summer. If you happen to be taking your vacation in the summer, obviously you can't visit Florida and Louisiana in the winter. Try the South in the summer. So long as you dress intelligently and refrain from athletics, it won't hurt you.

You might, however, be careful about sunbathing. The sun can be very strong and usually is. This warning needs only to be given once, since the results of the first indulgence will do more to put you off ever taking your clothes off again than any amount of paternal advice on my part. You feel as though your limbs are bursting. You ache all over. You are dizzy and sick. You cannot lie down except on raw, sore places, you cannot sleep and you cannot eat. When you sunbathe, use a little cream and a lot of intelligence.

I am told that you can die of sunburn. I can easily believe it, just as I now believe that you can die of thirst. There was a time when I thought that you had to have a mortal disease or be pierced to the heart or lose gallons of blood before you lay at death's door, but I have recently revised my opinions.

Go to Washington. If you dislike New York, you will like Washington, though it is easy to like both, and I suppose some people who are hard to please will dislike both. Anyway, it is quite different from New York. New York is piled high and noisy and youthful. It has little patience with age. It is raucous and wildly hilarious.

Washington has no sky-scrapers at all, but many palatial white buildings. Noise does not echo down narrow streets, but what noise there is is lost in the air, of which there seems to be more in Washington than in any other American city. It is quiet and spacious and dignified. All the great buildings are set in rich parks and wide green lawns. Nothing is crowded. The avenues are wide and space is plentiful.

And as for youth and age, the city is like a glorified Harrogate, Bath, Bournemouth and Leamington all in one. After New York it is strange to sit in a hotel lounge with dozens of dear old white-haired ladies knitting and chatting in soft southern accents. There seemed scarcely to be an old lady in New York, and if there were, she was probably in hiding and certainly not knitting.

Washington is clean and rather English and old-fashioned. There are the Buxton and

Matlock hydro ladies, and although the city is only a hundred and fifty years old it has an ancient and very lovely sense of maturity and restfulness. At your hotel, if it happens to be Christmas, there will be a carol service at which the coloured servants will sing Christmas carols and negro spirituals. The management will hang little stockings of candies on your bed and be charmingly playful and maternal in every way. If it is not Christmas you will be sure of being shown that famous southern hospitality which exists most acutely in that part of the South that borders on the North, but which is to be found, too, in the far South, especially in New Orleans and country districts.

If about once a year you permit yourself to be dragged out on a tourist expedition and sit in a rubberneck wagon, there is no better place to do it than Washington. In company with the ubiquitous affectionate couple, the eager-to-be-informed youths, the earnest middle-aged women who become coquettish with the guide and ask dozens of questions, and the sour suspicious ones who never quite believe what they are being told, you can cross the Potomac (stress on the second syllable, "toe-mack") into Alexandria, Va., and see George Washington's gloves, chair, portrait, Masonic apron, letters, penknife, medicine glass and small brass trowel.

Then, like a good American citizen, you

visit Mount Vernon. The house itself is beautiful and its setting exquisite. It is on a green hill, a white house with a little street of outhouses, spinning rooms, bakehouses and coachhouses, and around the Mount are trees —deciduous trees, lacy and leafless if it is winter, and evergreens thick and dark against the airy emptiness of the others. The whole Mount overlooks the Potomac River which sweeps around one splendid curve down towards Chesapeake Bay and the ocean. Both banks are green with lawns and woods, and the cypresses are clustered like little old people in dark green enveloping cloaks.

I drove across the state of Virginia three times, but the nearest I got to it was during a stay of a few days in a tiny village on the edge of the Blue Ridge Mountains.

Two interesting things happened on the way there. The bus in which I was travelling stopped at Culpeper and gave us fifteen minutes in which to refresh ourselves.

We all flocked into a café for coffee and raisin pie. A negress had been sitting in the back of the bus. When she entered the café, the proprietress shouted "You go out of here. I cain't serve you." So the negress went sorrowfully out and was given her portion at the back door. I had already noticed that every station had separate waiting rooms,

labelled "White" and "Colored." This was
new to me after living in the north.

My second stop was in Charlottesville, where
I stayed the night. As a town it was dull, and
its Main Street had the usual trolley cars,
three movie theatres and half a dozen drugstores crowded into the two hundred yards of
bright lights. But Charlottesville is a good
centre for the middle of Virginia, and it has
one of the loveliest university buildings in
America.

I spent the few days I had to spare in the
village of Yancey Mills. Yancey Mills had a
garage, a Baptist church and a tiny post office
and little else, except the place I stayed in
which was really a tourist cabin, but quite the
pleasantest and most luxurious of the breed.
It was a little white cottage with a bedroom
and a shower and a separate sitting room with
four chairs in it, two of them rockers. All
around were the Blue Ridge Mountains,
rustling with wind and squirrels and foxes and
covered with trees and pasture land. Cowbells
tinkled in the valley and a cow occasionally
wandered up to my cabin window.

I walked a part of each day, whatever the
weather. On fine days the Blue Ridge glowed
like grapes against the cloudless sky, and I
made more ambitious journeys. One day I
was driven to the foothills and then proceeded

to walk up the Ridge. I inquired the best way, but no one seemed to know except an old man at the post office of the tiny fruit growing settlement. They never bothered to climb the Ridge, he said. I followed his directions and after a while I came to a queer white cottage, the kind you read about in fairy tales. It was in a clearing, and at first I thought it was empty. The windows and doors were closed, but I saw as I came nearer that blue smoke was drifting lazily out of the chimney, blackened around its rim, and I heard noises inside, noises of plates rattling and the high voice of a child. But I saw no one at all. It looked the kind of place a witch might choose to live in. This particular witch had a Ford car instead of a broom, and for this reason would doubtless make far more terrifying noises in the darkness of the night.

I went on, up and up, through the woods, past a tinkling stream, over rough bridges made of rolled slim trunks of trees, and on away up to the open spaces above the trees, from where I could see the whole valley, yellow grey with sun and mist. It was hot climbing. I passed a sheet of ice on the way up, but at the top it was warm enough to sit down and let the January sun shine on me.

That winter was very mild. The next one was more severe and I had to go as far as

Florida before I could lie comfortably in the sun.

On a Saturday night in Connecticut in December I tramped out of my room shin deep in snow, lugging a suitcase. The streets were very treacherous since the old snow had caked underneath and was hard and slippery while the new snow was shivering down, filling the streets and rounding off thickly and whitely the sharp edged gables of the houses. The old campus of Yale looked beautiful with the lights in orange and yellow squares looking out on to the lacy white trees and the carpeted soft grass.

A taxi rescued me before I had tramped very far. The man drove fast, although we were in plenty of time, and in spite of his chains we skidded on the ice once or twice.

The midnight train was late and everyone was sleepy except a lively bunch of fellows who took it into their heads to bait an old red-nosed plump codger in the seat across the aisle from mine. They persisted in calling him Mr. Gilhooley, and when this failed to rouse him, Finnigan. He was probably not Irish at all, though he looked it and he reacted Irishly enough, much to the delight of the hooligans, who were possibly Irish themselves. They sang him Irish songs all the way from Bridgeport to Stamford, and one in particular annoyed

him more than any other, as well it might. It
went like this:

"Irishman, Irishman, bow down your head;
If I thought I was Irish I'd rather be dead.
Go over to Ireland and there you will see
How dirty and filthy the Irish can be."

It was after two o'clock in the morning when
our arrival at the Pennsylvania Station deliver-
ed him from their torments. Six hours later,
after a few hours' sleep I arrived again at the
Pennsylvania Station from my hotel to board
the Florida train. New York was piled thick
with snow, and machines were hacking it away
and piling it up in huge heaps along the streets
and avenues. The sky had cleared and it had
stopped snowing. Between the tall buildings
there were clear blue strips and a golden glow
in the south-east.

I settled myself in my train and saw nothing
but snow the whole day, through New Jersey,
Pennsylvania, Delaware, Maryland and Virginia, until I began to fear that the blizzard
had reached the West Indies. As I crept into
my berth in North Carolina, the fields and
woods were still white, and the snow lay thick
upon the railroad tracks.

I slept through South Carolina and Georgia
and woke up near Jacksonville, Florida, to find

all the snow gone and a dull, quiet day in progress.

I stayed one day at Saint Augustine. I had originally intended staying there a week, but it was Septemberish and I wanted June, so I boarded the train next day and went south for six hours and a half, by which time autumn had become midsummer and there was no mistaking it.

It seemed a little impertinent, when I was later checking latitudes on a map, for a Londoner to find Cairo too chilly and to move up the Nile to Assouan, but roughly speaking, that is how it was.

The familiar old friend the Gulf Stream makes all Florida south of Palm Beach as warm in the winter as California in the summer, and it was a comfortable feeling to slip almost perceptibly into summer as we rounded the little bump at Lake Worth Inlet some ten miles north of Palm Beach. On the way down we passed long groves of oranges, the fruit clustered thickly on trees ranging from three feet to twenty feet high. And grape fruit— round yellow globes shining schoolboy-like in the sun.

I stayed in a comfortable little hotel in Hollywood, Florida. Hollywood is on U.S. 1, the highway that runs the entire length of the Atlantic coast. In boom days it was a thriving little resort and will doubtless be the same again, but as things were in the winter of 1932-3, I was almost the only visitor in the place. I was shown pictures of Hollywood in 1925 and I preferred it as it was in the depression. I stayed within a mile of the sea and did almost nothing. My hotel was a long flat two-storey building and I was its only guest. The motherly, white haired lady who was in charge instantly adopted me and became very friendly. I had no meals in the hotel, but went to a house next door for two meals a day, a large breakfast and a large five o'clock dinner, which I ate with the family. I took my lunch out, either at a little café near the beach or at the café attached to the service station on U.S. 1, and it generally consisted of a salad, a glass of milk and a piece of pie. For breakfast I had papaya, which I had never eaten before. It was served with half a lime and tasted like a delicate variety of honeydew melon.

The hotel had one little lounge, which the manageress and I shared, and when I came indoors each evening after spending the whole day in the sun, we sat and talked or glanced at the news of the day while the radio tinkled gently in a corner. Occasionally, visitors dropped in, and I was always introduced. Once the owners of the hotel came to visit the manageress. They were very wealthy, she had whispered to me, Scandinavians they were, from the Middle West. Like most Middle Westerners they were simple, unaffected and friendly, and immediately invited me to visit them at their home a short distance away and take dinner one evening.

Before they came I had already become friendly with their handy man, a rosy Dane of about thirty-five. He it was who looked after the garden and drove a dilapidated truck around Hollywood. He was one of the friendliest people I have ever met. He was a bachelor and a socialist and a wide reader. He had worked in Greenland and showed me many pictures of his life there.

He asked me whether I should like to see his little house and collection of books. I said I should, so one afternoon he drove me in his amazing little truck to a small cabin where he kept his treasures, all of which he proudly showed me.

The last evening I spent in Hollywood he came to talk with me again and to say goodbye. He was a cheerful little man, with sandy hair and laughing blue eyes, and he wore, every time I saw him, a white linen suit and a white linen cap, except once when he was operating his truck, when he wore blue jeans. He had been well off some years ago, but all his property had been destroyed in a hurricane, and he had had to begin all over again.

For ten days I lived the lazy life of sitting outside in the sunshine, except when the sun got too hot, with a soft breeze coming up from the sea and the palm leaves rustling. And when the wind dropped it became very hot indeed and the spiky leaves of the palms spread themselves fanlike against the blue of the sky.

Opposite my little courtyard where I sat daily was the local golf course. It had a palm-fringed club house in a pinkish cream colour, a squat, red tiled tower and two balconies that just asked to be used in a production of "Romeo and Juliet" or "The Two Gentlemen of Verona." Even the drain pipes were beautiful, pale green and neat, matching the pale green woodwork around the windows. Each morning an old nigger wearing a straw hat swept the dust off the sidewalk with a long whisk broom.

I let myself slide gently into the slow rhythm of the place. In the next garden fifty yards away sat two old men in white shirts reading their newspapers near a banana tree. My only exertion was to walk a mile down to the beach, swim a little, lie in the sun, and walk back along the white roads cut through the swampy wilderness, past long low houses with red tiled roofs and little Spanish towers and windows and balconies. Nine hours out of ten the sky was bright blue, and the houses were white or grey or buff or cream or pale terracotta, in fact all the colours that look best against sky-blue. The hour of no sunshine consisted of sharp downpours of rain, only ten to fifteen minutes in duration each. One afternoon I was caught in one of these showers as I walked back from the beach. The dark cloud came suddenly, the wind lashed, and the rain fell, hissing and leaping. The cloud glided away, the sun shone warmly, the roads steamed, and in another fifteen minutes all was as it had been before.

When I walked to the beach I never met anyone. One day as I stepped on to the sand I saw a woman and two children leaving the beach some distance away, but otherwise I had the whole beach to myself. I was told that I should find people if I went half a mile in a northerly direction, but I never went.

When I left my hotel bill was one dollar a day, and my two meals, ninety-five cents.

One spring I drove to Charleston, South Carolina. It was too early to see the flowers at their best, but the gardens were beautiful even before they were in full season.

After most American cities, Charleston seems very old and European with its great houses, twisted iron gates and flaming azaleas. People who know the South will tell you that Charleston is not what it was. I am ready to believe that it has changed a great deal and not for the better, but if you do not know what the lamented old Charleston was like, the new Charleston will seem old and very charming after you have been staying or living in a thoroughly modern, fast moving northern city.

I stayed for a few days in a decaying inn on Meeting Street. There was a modern hotel a few blocks away, but the inn had been recommended to me, and I knew that the modern hotel would be just as at home in California or Indiana as in South Carolina. The inn was dingy and old fashioned, but had clearly seen far better days. It had a tremendous veranda on which I spent many hours, looking down the street and listening to the rain. When it was sunny I walked around the city or drove.

My room was on a corner of the rambling old building and had a bathroom attached. The bath water came out of the tap the colour of soup but the decoration of the room was lordly. Instead of the usual parchment walls and moderately pleasing prints of a modern hotel, two of my walls were entirely window, ornamented graciously with white painted wood and discreetly hung with thin curtains. The other two walls held the utilities, two doors, the bed and a wardrobe. The dressing-table was placed diagonally at the junction of the two window walls. In this way the room was satisfactorily divided. As you lay or sat up in bed you seemed to be in a lavish apartment. When you stepped into the lavishness you tried not to look back at the huddled and gloomy necessities. Hotel rooms are not now built with such extremes of outlook, though the general standard is higher.

I moved on for three or four days to Summerville, some twenty miles out of Charleston and a little self-conscious of its garden quality. It was in Summerville that I felt nearest to the South as the early colonial families must have known it.

The house was old and rambling, and its peace was the greater for the garden that lay around it. Underfoot were pine needles of a couple of decades, and when the garden came to an end at the gates there was no hard surfaced road but merely a sandy lane, so that the only noises came from within the house, and they were the pleasant crackle of burning logs, the tinkle of crockery at meal times, and the soft chatter of the negro servants.

My room was at the end of a long passage and had three windows which I could open wide to the moonlit night and the scented trees. From the tall pines hung long festoons of grey Spanish moss that looked ghostly by night and

even by day a little unearthly as they swayed
slowly and seemed to breathe.

Each morning a negro boy would come in
and close my windows and light a fragrant fire
of pitch pine for me to dress by.

When it was time for me to return north, I
took a wide curving route that led me through
Savannah and the great swamp country of the
southern lowlands, inland up the Savannah
river into the Blue Ridge Mountains of North
Carolina. Asheville is the centre of this region.
Some of the loveliest and wildest country east
of the Rockies is within easy reach of Asheville.
A road cutting right across the Great Smoky
Mountains has recently been paved, and the
mountain pass that coils up from Tennessee
and meets North Carolina on the very ridge
of this great range is as breathtaking as anything
in America. These two states alone are worth
weeks of exploring in their variety. They join
several thousand feet high, indistinguishable
from each other, the one stretching east to the
Atlantic and the loneliness of Nag's Head and
the other west to the Mississippi River.

From Chapel Hill, N.C. where I stayed at
the charming Carolina Inn, I did my greatest
driving feat, that of driving alone five hundred
and fifty miles to the centre of New York City
in one day. When I started I had no intention
of driving to New York, but it was a sunny day

and my little Chevrolet seemed to be running as smoothly as she had ever run in her life, and it seemed no great distance to Washington. My intention was to stay in Philadelphia for the night, and drive on to New York in the morning. A few miles south-west of Baltimore I stopped in a roadside café for some bacon and eggs, coffee and apple-pie. As I sat there eating it, four elderly ladies entered to drink some coffee and eat some pie also.

"How far are we from New York?" asked one of them.

"About two hundred miles," answered the café proprietor.

"Is that all?" exclaimed the elderly lady, and then turned to the others.

"We can make it easy," she explained, "you don't want to get to bed before twelve o'clock, do you?"

"Oh, no," the others chorused, "that'll be fine"

"Where've you folks come from?" asked the proprietor.

"Why, we just started out of Savannah early this morning," chirped the eldest.

For a second I hoped it was a joke, but it wasn't. They had driven from Savannah and they were going to New York. As I paid my bill I peeped at them. The youngest was some thirty years my senior. I walked out and I drove to New York.

It was June when I drove through the South from Maryland to Mexico. There were four of us in two small cars, and we carried camp beds in the rumble seats. The rain which came to save the corn and the tobacco crops interfered with our camping prospects, but we managed one night on a grassy hill in Virginia and one night in an Alabama cotton field.

The night in Virginia was our first attempt and we were all secretly longing to put off the wild life and sleep in a hotel that night, but each determined not to be the first to suggest such a backsliding. So we slept out. We followed a lonely little road and had much difficulty in selecting a suitable spot, none of us knowing exactly what a camp site in Virginia should look like. With mosquitoes well in mind we finally dragged our camp beds up a hill and spread them out on a pleasant plot of smooth grass. The stars were glowing thickly, and there was a pale moon behind the clouds that drifted over near the horizon. Above, it was clear. The air was warm and the katydids (cicalas) were chirping in the trees. As we got into our pyjamas and slipped between the blankets we could see hosts of fireflies flitting silently across the meadow and flashing pale green lights against the dark of the trees.

Five cows sauntered up the hill and stood

around, watching our proceedings with interest. After a few unsuccessful attempts to chew our blankets they gave up and went on pleasantly cropping grass all around us until we fell asleep. From the heat of the early evening it grew cold in the middle of the night, and I found it necessary to wriggle into a thick woollen sweater, slip on a pair of socks and snuggle more closely into the blankets.

The days seemed very hot, and at Abingdon, Virginia, we invested twenty-five cents each in wide brimmed hats of straw. These we afterwards found a great comfort, and we wore them very often, except in the cities.

From Big Stone Gap, in the Cumberland Mountains, we went into a coal mine. The little village was called Appalachia. We were dragged half a mile into a mountain on a noisy, rattling truck, until we were seventeen hundred feet below the surface of the ground. Then someone hacked at the coal face and we had the joyful terror of hearing the loose rock crackling above our heads. We had to walk bent half double for a long way. It was painful and very hot.

A house in Abingdon advertised home cooking and we had our evening meal there. The owner of the house was inordinately proud of her cooking and produced baked ham, corn on the cob and sweet potatoes for us. In the centre of the huge round table was a revolving dumb waiter on which were butter, condiments, and dishes of Southern hot biscuits.

Similar meals, as good or nearly as good, but none better, may be had throughout the South. Sometimes the notice "Home Cooking" leads you to an excellent meal; sometimes you are disappointed. You must take your chance.

West of Abingdon we stopped for lunch at an old farmhouse that had a spinning-wheel of which it was proud, a moose horn and an ancient four-poster bed. From the side of the bed a large drawer pulled out into which they used to put the babies to sleep, leaving the drawer open, of course.

The night we drove into Kentucky there was a violent thunderstorm. When the rain stopped we opened our windows again. The smell of clover and honeysuckle blew freshly from the fields and hedges, and as the clouds passed, the moon glowed from between them and shone on the hills and trees and the scattering of white wooden houses.

In Tennessee, at the foot of the Great Smoky Mountains, we found a wooden cabin of five rooms so pleasantly situated that we decided to stay there a few days. We subsisted on simple meals with the exception of evening dinner which we cooked ourselves with the aid of a mysterious and dangerous looking oil stove which once burst into a sudden blaze but did no material damage. The cooking was a confused business. What with four unpractised cooks in the tiny kitchen at the same time and a raging thunderstorm among the mountains that caused the lights to fail periodically and for long· and inconvenient stretches of time, it was surprising that we achieved anything at all.

In the neighbouring village of Gatlinburg, where we shopped, they had an old barn which was devoted to entertainment and social pursuits. One night they had a wrestling match between an Indian from one of the North Carolina reservations and a white man, and an excited crowd surged around. There were no ropes, and the wrestlers occasionally hurled each other into our midst. After the wrestling a dozen young people danced a couple of Virginia Reels. A trio wearing Mexican hats and floral trousers played slightly out of tune and sang raucously but in strict rhythm and the dancers obviously enjoyed every minute of it. One of the tunes they played was the favourite "She'll be comin' round the mountain."

Almost outside our front door was Mount Le Conte, one of the highest peaks in eastern North America, somewhere between six and seven thousand feet high. It was forested to the summit and not at all like a Scotch or

Swiss mountain. The views through clearings showed us ridge upon ridge of forested mountain in immense serried rows. It was hot climbing, but there was a waterfall half-way up to cool us, and on the top it was chilly.

By the time we decided to walk down again, great clouds had gathered and a thunderstorm was clearly preparing to burst. We were half-way down before the rain came, but if we had been within two minutes of the bottom we should have got just as wet. It was pleasant to have that abandoned feeling of not having to care where we trod, since we were quickly soaked to saturation point and had no need to step delicately. The narrow path became a rushing stream, and we just walked through the water, slushing on for miles, the water almost up to our knees, while the lightning flashed and the thunder roared and the rain screamed and pelted. When we got to our cabin we were too wet to go inside, so we stripped off our clothes on the porch and darted in for a vigorous towelling and a supper of bacon and eggs, sweet potatoes and peaches.

This little sojourn in Tennessee was followed by a hurried dash across Georgia, Alabama, Mississippi and Louisiana to New Orleans, so that my memory of these states is a vagueness of little towns, negroes, and cottonfields. Gainsville, Ga., I remember as having the

worst tourist house I stayed at in the entire
United States. Atlanta, Ga., seemed bustling
enough, and very hot. Mobile, Alabama, impressed me considerably. It was my conception of the South and the kind of city I had
been looking for all the way from the southernmost tip of Virginia. There is a sub-tropical
warmth and richness about Mobile and the
same slow smoothness that you feel in New
Orleans itself. I noted both of them as cities
to be revisited.

New Orleans is a study in itself. Whether
your great joy is to eat bananas on the dockside, to gaze at Maya exhibits in Tulane
University Museum, to peep into the old
French courtyards or to eat at Antoine's, you
will remember New Orleans and everything
you did there from the first moment you
entered Canal Street to the last when the
Mississippi ferry takes you west on your way
to Texas. And if you wander tactfully along
the back streets at night you may come across
a negro religious meeting in full progress.

If you go into Texas, most of your time will
be spent in getting out of it again. If you want
to stay there, stay in San Antonio, which is as
successful a mixture of old and new as anything in the United States. Texas is so large
that it spills into the South, the Middle West
and the West. Over the Rio Grande is Mexico,

and Texas itself borders against such widely different states as Louisiana, Arkansas, Oklahoma and New Mexico.

The people of eastern Texas speak with a rich Southern accent, and the state ranks first in the production of cotton. But in spite of the drawl and the cottonfields, Texas has little of that flavour that makes a southern state part of the South. Like Florida it seems not to belong, and once you are over the Mississippi River, you are in country that has little in common with Georgia and the Carolinas. You are, in fact, in the easternmost and southernmost part of that enormous region called the West.

The West is, to many travellers, a series of fifteen National Parks with a scattering of National monuments.

You can read about the National parks in a book published by the United States Department of the Interior and called the National Parks Portfolio. You can also drive to them and stay in them. Many Americans spend their entire summer in a National Park or flit up and down the country from one park to another. As you would expect, the parks cover the show places of the Rocky Mountains and the Sierras, but to do them justice, they are so extensive in area that only certain restricted parts of them are crowded and vulgarized. Accommodations range from the prescribed camping sites to comfortable hotels. If your time is limited, it is better to stay in one park only, any one of them, and ride or walk or drive in it, rather than to see merely the populous core of each of the fifteen.

If you are in the habit of camping-out, you may do this only on the prescribed camping sites. If these do not attract you, you had better choose some spot outside the boundaries of the park or sleep in a cabin or hotel.

It is possible that you will dislike the National Park system and be glad to get out into ordinary country again. We all agree that advertisements and haphazard building developments are hideous, and we welcome laws that protect the countryside, but somehow we resent the fact that such laws are necessary when we see references to them posted up impersonally and not sensing the difference between us who know how to behave ourselves and the people who don't. We should like the notices to apologize in some way, to disappear into a tree or bob three times or something. We are still selfish enough to prefer the places that are untouched because no one had discovered them to those that owe their sanctity to the all-seeing eye and avenging hand of the United States Department of the Interior.

It is a distressing symptom, but the aversion to sharing with strangers is deep-seated, and deeper-seated in the British than in the Americans.

My recollections of western life are mostly associated with places outside the National Parks, except for one occasion in Glacier Park when we drove to the top of a long pass and walked some distance. We crossed a ridge which echoed and sparkled with glacier streams, and then suddenly we saw a valley. Opposite was a craggy mountain with patches of snow on its grey-green sides. Around this mountain in a magnificent curve swept a lake, joining a glacier and a torrent. On the lake were little green promontories and islands with stiff, dark green fir trees standing sharply against the fresh light green of the grass. At one end the lake was the colour of a black olive, and it gradually became lighter and bluer. Where it disappeared into its torrent two slopes of fir trees met, and beyond that there was just slope after slope and ridge after ridge of blue mountain flecked with crannies of snow. And out of an almost cloudless sky the sun shone, and a cool breeze brought the scent of the sun soaked cypresses up the long pass.

I picked some green needles of a fragrant shrub I found growing among the rocks and put them inside a letter which I later des-

T—a

patched to London. I thought of its changing
trains at Chicago, being shipped at New York
and finally falling with a plop on a London
door-mat, and I wondered whether it would
keep its strong fresh scent. Two years and a
half later I was shown the letter. A piece of the
dried needle had stuck fast between two sheets
of paper and the scent came to me at the distance of a foot and brought back the vision of
the whole scene, the warmth of the sun and the
feel of the wind.

We drove down the winding pass in a glow of
happiness and extravagantly treated ourselves
to a dollar-fifty dinner at the hotel on Lake
McDonald, a huge log-cabin building with
Indian rugs of bright colours on the floor and
walls and a gigantic wood fire at one end.
The dining-room overlooks the lake, but
between is a garden of delphiniums, and you
may see a humming-bird quivering as it sucks
out the pollen with its needle beak and darts
from flower to flower. Its meat, however, is
not nectar, but the tiny insects that crawl
inside the trumpets of flowers.

We rented a hut with a stove in it by the side
of Lake McDonald and cooked our break-
fasts and lunches. Not far from our hut and
near the entrance to the park was one of the
most eloquent public notices I have ever seen.
In the middle of the rich woodland there was

a patch of desolation, where only a few young firs had started to sprout. On a withered tree trunk was the simple statement: "There was a forest fire here in 1912."

The water of the lake was very cold, as you might expect in Glacier Park. No one ever stayed in the water for long. I swam in it once. As I came out of the water, stiff with cold, I was suddenly attacked by a small dog. Its mistress apologized profusely, explaining that she had ordered it to go into the water after a fish, but that it had come for me instead. I didn't feel flattered. However, I consoled myself by sun-bathing and watching the water ripple in the gentle wind and listening to it lap against the sides of two little terra-cotta boats.

Even so, my memory of Montana is sharper and clearer of the Flathead lake country, and of one early morning in particular when I rolled off my camp-bed in the middle of the forest at dawn and walked out of the shady undergrowth into the greenish gold of the newly risen sun on the trees.

The chief trouble with the West is its size. If you like mountains, concentrate on Montana and Colorado, if you like loneliness, try Wyoming, for Indians stay in New Mexico and Arizona, for deserts Utah and Nevada, and for Hollywood and the bathing beaches, California. California also has mountains, loneliness, Indians and deserts, but none of the other western states have Hollywood.

After days of sun-blasted deserts you suddenly come' into the scurry and brilliance of Los Angeles. No wonder you go quite mad when you are in it. This city is breathless. It is almost a crime to drive at less than thirty-five miles an hour in its streets. You pelt along at forty or fifty and race a dozen gleaming cars to the next block. The whole place is alive with a sort of theatrical magnetism. The sun and the Pacific Ocean together make you feel utterly reckless and abandoned. The boulevards are wide and smooth and everything seems to have been planned for ease and speed and richness.

Hollywood has been so much talked about, and occupies so unwarrantedly large a place in any European's conception of America that I think we can put it in its proper place and dispense with it briefly.

You will want, of course, to see inside a studio, preferably several of the larger studios, but unless you provide yourself with introductions or happen to know someone in Hollywood, you will find some difficulty in entering. There are notices displayed stating that visitors are strictly forbidden, but once you are a guest, you slip right in and everyone is as charming as you could hope, including the bored actors themselves. You will probably wonder how they can achieve anything at all in the conditions under which they work, and you will observe that in almost every instance the acting is pretty bad. However, you will enjoy seeing the familiar faces around the lots, and you will spend more time peeping nonchalantly from table to table than eating salad in the sensible and inexpensive studio cafés.

As usual I did the wrong things in Hollywood, or the right things at the wrong time, which is worse. On the night of a movie première, when I should have dutifully paid five dollars and fifty cents for a seat in the Egyptian Theatre, I was on my way to the Hollywood Bowl to listen to a concert. We were driving along the Hollywood Boulevard and with us were rank upon rank of cars, a brilliant assembly, waiting to get near enough to the theatre to step out. Five searchlights played on the roof of the theatre, and the crowd seemed to have no end. We eventually got through and to our concert where we sat beneath the moon with a soft breeze drifting up from the Pacific and listened to Beethoven's Fifth Symphony.

The two great cities of California are hated rivals and they stand to each other very much in the same relation as Boston and New York on the Atlantic coast. San Francisco is the older and likes to think of itself as cultured and more beautiful as opposed to the untidy, widely scattered, go-ahead mushroom growth that is Los Angeles.

According to the San Franciscans, the Southern Californians suffer badly from megalomania. Los Angeles is ridiculed for its apparent desire to incorporate every village near or far within its city line. Driving through the desert among the outskirt settlements, you suddenly see a notice saying "Los Angeles City Line." There is a tale told by northerners that the last thing you see coming out of Honolulu harbour is a little board sticking out of the water announcing "Los Angeles City Line."

In 1906 San Francisco had its great earthquake. Los Angeles made much of this and laughed at the San Franciscan habit of claiming that the damage done was almost all by fire and that only very little was by earthquake. Then Los Angeles had an earthquake of its own and beneath their sympathy the San Franciscans were delighted. For a while the Southerners were embarrassed. Then someone wrote to a newspaper to ask which was the bigger earthquake, the one at San Francisco or the one at Los Angeles. Los Angeles suddenly had an idea. No longer did it feel defeated and ashamed. It claimed the bigger earthquake and once more the rival city was snubbed.

San Francisco is built on forty-nine hills, seven times as many as ancient Rome, and some of its streets are alarmingly steep. Drive up Jones Street or Mason Street and look back as you near the top.

There are no elevated railways or subways in San Francisco. Their place is taken by trolley cars, and some of the hills have to have cogs.

There is a story of a trolley car that slipped its cogs on one of the steep hills and began to back down, much to the terror of the occupants. A taxi driver behind it tried valiantly to get his cab out of the way but failed and at the last instant leaped to safety, leaving his taxi on the track. The car crashed into the taxi and its momentum being arrested the whole wreckage came to a gentle standstill and caused no further damage.

The witnesses acclaimed the taxi driver, who, they asserted, had deliberately sacrificed his taxi so that the trolley car would not crash down into the busy square below and cause several unpleasant accidents.

The taxi driver held his peace and became the hero of San Francisco. The point is, how did the story get around? Did the taxi driver confess in his cups, or was the whole thing the invention of a Southern Californian?

Both cities have a Chinatown, San Francisco's being the more famous. Chinatown is one of the sights of San Francisco and is a confusion of rabbits, jade, ducks, ivory, chicken, lacquer, tea, incense, lichee nuts and tobacco. Many of its stores cater rather obviously for the tourist and large quantities of worthless junk are sold, but if you go there with a San Franciscan who knows the district well you can obtain some excellent things. Very few now wear Chinese costume, and I saw no young people in anything but the most ordinary and serviceable American clothes.

One of the most attractive quarters of San Francisco is Fisherman's Wharf. It is like a bit of Naples with its rust-coloured nets, blue and white boats, its smell of fish, gleam of scales, seagulls and fishermen. One morning I saw two Italian fishermen eating bread and olives out of a folded napkin neatly perched between them. Near by bobbed little boats, San Giuseppe, Maria and Gesu Bambino.

While you are in San Francisco you might look at the Civic Centre and the Opera House. A very intelligent and cultivated negro will take you over the Opera House and will explain it all with a real pride.

If you like tropical fish, there is an aquarium

in Golden Gate Park, and if you enjoy shopping, San Francisco can give you all you want, its bookstores being particularly good.

Drive over the Twin Peaks and along the Skyline Boulevard and have a look at the two universities, Stanford at Palo Alto, and Berkeley across the Bay. And Berkeley is Burkeley, not Barclay.

You will appreciate the climate of San Francisco if you have crossed the great plains and the deserts in a small open car. It is pleasant to wear almost nothing and frizzle, but after a month or two of it, there is something to be said for a city in which you can wear an ordinary suit and walk around the town in midsummer without feeling hot and washed-out. No one in San Francisco looks thirsty and damp and worn, as a great many people look in the summer from New York west, north to Canada and south to the Gulf. Even if you like the heat and it has not bothered you unduly, you feel refreshed in San Francisco. You had better put away your white linen suit in this city. It offends them to see you wearing tropical clothing in a cool climate.

Santa Barbara is a hundred miles from Los Angeles and three hundred and fifty from San Francisco, but it is decidedly San Franciscan in sentiment. In spite of its efforts to be charming, it actually is charming. It is a pity that it tries so hard and so self-consciously to be Spanish. It looks quite Spanish enough without parading its fiesta and calling State Street Estado Street. However, it is the tourists and the Chamber of Commerce that arrange these things between them. The natives of Santa Barbara care little one way or the other. They are mostly old and more interested in their bath chairs than in mounting Spanish steeds to celebrate the early days of California. There is an air of prosperous ill-health about Santa Barbara. Some of the wealthy estates of Montecito are lovely to look at, but the humbler people shake their heads over the lonely old Crœsuses and tell stories of how one is mentally deranged, another a grief stricken widower, a third a cripple, and a fourth recently separated from his spouse. Being a millionaire, apparently, solves only some of life's problems.

If you are specially interested in Indian and Spanish American life you should spend some time in Arizona and New Mexico. You may be fortunate in discovering a little known village, but you will more probably buy your Indian rugs in company with middle-class America furnishing its home, and you will observe that as soon as the white man makes an appearance, the Indian women spread their pottery in rows outside their dwellings. It all seems very cheap, this parading of the once noble redskin, and you will doubtless be glad to move on to more honest and less self-conscious places. The Indian reservations are neither the West that was nor the West that is, except within their boundaries. The Indians I saw in North Carolina and Canada seemed much happier in their blue shirts and duck pants than these showcase models in the South West.

If you stay in Sante Fé or Taos you might drive through the local Spanish villages. The roads are narrow and precipitous and appalling in every way and you will probably stick in the sand, but their very inaccessibility makes these villages well worth seeing.

Small towns and cities are much the same in the West as elsewhere.

If you are undecided whether to go to Salt Lake City or Denver and you cannot go to both, go to Denver.

Salt Lake City has an organ on which sentimental and thoroughly bad music is constantly being played, and a lake in which you cannot swim. You can put on a bathing suit and sit or lie or stand in it, but that can hardly be called swimming. The Great Salt Lake makes you feel very foolish and it gets in your eyes and nostrils and makes them smart,

and as you walk out you find yourself all en-
crusted, like dried seaweed.

Denver is different.

On the map it looks almost among the
Rockies. Actually, the mountain peaks are
visible from the road by which you enter
Denver from Cheyenne, and Denver is called
the "Queen City of the Plains," not very
often, fortunately, and then only in writing.

Denver is a mile high and very healthy. The
Daniels and Fisher Store has a tower modelled
after the tower in the Piazza San Marco,
Venice, and though its setting is not so beautiful as the Venetian, it does not look ridi-
culously out of place, but lends quite a dignified air to the otherwise commonplace
street.

One evening in Denver I went to Elitch's
Park. The taxi that drove me there went as
furiously as any vehicle I have known. On this
account the pleasant portals of Elitch's Park
seemed all the more safe and inviting. I had
no idea what kind of a place it was. All I knew
was that it advertised the performance of a
play I wanted to see.

It turned out to be an amusement park
resembling the eighteenth century pleasure
gardens much more than an English fair.
There were hedges and flowers and a delicately lighted colonnade. There were the usual

adjuncts to a fair, a calliope, a shooting-range, and similar attractions, but the people seemed very well dressed and almost perfectly behaved.

There was no rowdyism and no apparent vulgarity. There are those who would say that such a fair is a milk-livered, suburban affair, and that fairs should be rowdy, screeching and sweaty. I agree. But all the same there was something delightfully Victorian and demure about this very respectable amusement park. In my naïveté I may have invested Elitch's gardens with an innocence it never possessed, but that was the impression it gave me.

There were little cafés among the trees, glimmering with sedate "garden party" lights. People were quietly drinking lemonade in some and beer in others. I drank some Milwaukee beer and it was very good.

There was a large, open-air covered dance floor. Lanterns hung around with three glass plates in each window reading respectively One Step, Waltz and Foxtrot. As each dance was about to begin, the light was switched on to shine through whichever section of glass it should.

Close to the dance hall was the theatre, a summer garden theatre, with white cloths tied to the seats. Nearly everyone was dressed in white and since the theatre was full, it was a pleasing sight.

The safety curtain looked familiar—a Warwickshire cottage, thatched roof, and a section
of English lane. Beneath the picture was the
rhyme:

"Ann Hathaway's cottage a mile away
    Shakespeare sought at close of day."

The play we saw was "One Sunday Afternoon," a gentle and charming piece of work
about the Middle West from 1904 onwards.
It dealt largely with parks and beer gardens
and was therefore singularly appropriate to
Elitch's garden theatre. Moreover, it was well
directed and acted.

The next night we saw more Victorian cos-
tumes on stage, this time in the famous musical
play "The Merry Widow" performed at the
Central City Opera House.

I should have known all about Central City,
but it was only a few hours preceding the
evening performance that I discovered that
this theatre was fifty miles or so out of Denver.
I had gone on the assumption, an appallingly
ignorant one, that Central City was an old
name for Denver itself. When I discovered my
mistake I argued that I was not utterly and
shamefully wrong, since Central City was the
capital of Colorado before Denver, and Denver
had another name once, but it was Auralia,
not Central City. On reflection, this does not
make a very good excuse, but it satisfied me at

the time. It even satisfied my companion who had to go without his dinner and fetch his car out of the garage when he had contemplated as easy an evening as that spent in Elitch's Park.

We were told to allow two hours for getting to Central City. We allowed the two hours and arrived just before the curtain rose. We had hoped to arrive in time to eat, since we had eaten merely a salad lunch and snatched a hasty cup of tea in the afternoon, but we had to go without.

We drove west on a good road which became not so good but very picturesque as we approached Idaho Springs. We crossed a mountain pass and went through a canyon with a river close by. It was growing dark and the moon shone on the river.

At Idaho Springs we turned sharply north into the mountains. There seemed nothing but a barrier, but somehow the road, a narrow track, struck valiantly and steeply against the barrier and began to wriggle cautiously up it.

After what seemed miles of climbing on a most precarious road we found ourselves at the top of the barrier and going down instead of up. Presently we saw Central City, a cluster of bright lights on the mountainside.

It seems that the discovery of gold in Colorado in 1859 was responsible for Central City and the other mining villages of this section of the Rockies, and that they were not only mining villages as we know them, but places of culture and revelry. Money was spent most lavishly and the Teller House, now a ramshackle inn, was a gathering place for ladies and gentlemen of charm and importance.

Central City was a thriving little community until the nineties. Then mining almost ceased and the cities dwindled until the census of 1930 gave Central City 572 inhabitants and Black Hawk 253. Nevadaville is given in that census as having a total population of two.

In Bartholomew's Pocket Gazetteer of 1892 published in London, Central City and Black Hawk were considered important enough for inclusion, their populations being respectively 2026 and 1540. Neither Hollywood nor Pasadena is mentioned in that edition.

In 1932 the Central City Opera House was re-opened for summer festival purposes, and going to it for the first time gives you the thrill you would get if you discovered a mountain pass on 42nd Street. Central City is on my re-visiting list in capital letters.

Just as cities are a welcome relief after weeks of deserts and plains and mountains and villages, so it is a good feeling to drive west into loneliness again after a short bout of neat clothes, modern hotels, shops and entertainments.

After a few days of Denver and Colorado Springs we were quite ready to face the Rocky Mountains and the desert wastes beyond.

Colorado Springs is a holiday resort, and you can have a pleasant time there. The Antlers Hotel is quite attractive and very reasonable in price, and there is the Broadmoor farther out if you do not want to be in town. The Broadmoor has an open-air swimming pool, and since Colorado is on the same latitude as Asia Minor, open-air swimming is a popular summer occupation. In the town there is the more humble Y.M.C.A. pool, not open-air, but containing enough water to swim in. If you cannot spare a couple of hours and do not want to lie in the sun, the indoor pool is close and handy.

You can ride or drive as much as you wish around Colorado Springs. Pike's Peak is near by, and the Pike National Forest, from which you can see miles and miles over the rolling plains of eastern Colorado. And to the west and sometimes all around you have scented forests and mountains, streams and canyons, and all the advertised attractions of the Rockies.

It is a pity that resorts quickly become vulgarized, but, looking at it in another light, it is good that the vulgarization is concentrated. For every small tourist town or dump of gas stations and cabins and cafés, there are miles of clear country. Manitou, a little outside Colorado Springs, advertises a Cave of the Winds and a Garden of the Gods, and if you like that sort of thing, there it is for you in Manitou, together with information bureaus, Kozy kabins, hot dog stands, flags and advertisements. You cannot miss the place, which I suppose is to its credit.

The Continental Divide is about a hundred miles west of Colorado Springs. The road was, in August 1933, and may still be, appalling. It had a wash-board or corduroy surface, and was the shakiest and most treacherous stretch of grit I have ever experienced.

About forty miles the other side of the Divide is Gunnison, a town of about fifteen hundred inhabitants. Gunnison, like Central, is a "ghost" city. It has a wide main street with no paving, a few one storey buildings and a few lights. Beyond that, and its population, of whom I saw only ten or fifteen, it has nothing but its memories.

We ate a meal in a typical Main Street café, the kind of meal you can eat from Idaho to Georgia, soup or tomato juice cocktail, roast pork, sweet potatoes, corn on the cob, pie or ice-cream, milk or coffee. We inquired about hotels, and they recommended the "La Veta," a little off Main Street at the west end of town.

It was an amazing building, dim with past glories. The lobby was enormous, and we followed a guide up a wide flight of stairs with massive wooden banisters and a gaudy blue and gold lamp stand, once oil or gas but now converted to electricity. Our room was forty feet long and thirteen feet wide. Great double doors opened into it from the hallway, and at the other end were two raised doors, the bottom about eighteen inches above the floor. These doors were glass panelled and one of them had steps for the ladies. They opened on to a spacious balcony with seats and a little fountain.

In this room were three huge wooden beds, the headpieces of solid wood, about four feet square and quite attractively carved. Between two of the beds was a heating radiator connected with a long pipe which disappeared into the ceiling. The walls were painted cream, but both ceiling and walls were blistering badly. The carpet showed signs of wear. The fireplace was of heavy marble, with a mirror six feet high set into the wall above the mantelpiece. There were two chairs, two tables and two chests of drawers. Near the fireplace was a tiny washstand with two taps.

I wondered what silver kings had slept in these great beds, men from the north and east and south, scraping silver and gold out of the gently smiling hills around. Fifty years ago, Gunnison showed promise of being a great city. On this promise, this lavish hotel was built, and everyone was very gay and extra-vagant. Then something happened, just as it happened in Central, the rich men went, or became poor men, the ladies followed. There were no more parties or balls or great feasts in the La Veta, and Gunnison fell away to noth-ing. The great hotel remained as it was, an empty, florid shell, echoing dismally of adven-ture and polkas.

The La Veta hotel advertises a free meal for every guest on any day when the sun fails to shine. Its guests are not numerous at any time, and sunless days in Colorado are even less numerous, as you can see if you read the large notice in the lobby which shows that in about twenty years many of these years had sunshine every day in that part of Colorado. In some of these years, the sun failed to shine on one day, and in one or two unfortunate years, the hotel, if it kept up this practice faithfully, had to feed its guests a free meal on two days in the year. No London hotel, I believe, can be persuaded into inaugurating such a charming custom. But then, London is not between seven and eight thousand feet above sea-level and eight hundred miles from the sea.

Outside, the La Veta hotel as I saw it the

following day, is a florid affair, decorated in two main colours, a purplish chocolate and a dirty cream. It has two stoops with doorways on either side of the main great entrance, and two verandas.

The store opposite is now a sad looking ruin with one modern advertisement pasted on its side.

During the night I heard the banging of doors echoing sadly through the huge corridors and thought of waltzing silks and gleaming silver and the old days. I remembered Hatasis, the mummy in the Toronto museum, her strong teeth, little nose, and golden brown hair. The glory of Gunnison and Central is as dead as Hatasis, although no doubt dozens of the belles of the silver West are still alive to-day, silent and dreaming, or garrulous old ladies sitting on suburban porches in Pasadena.

The West is changing, but it is still the battlefield of life and death, of industry and desolation.

I drove south two hundred miles through eastern Wyoming to Cheyenne. The road was bad, and there was nothing except rolling prairie for miles and miles and miles, a grey green and tawny land of sagebrush and a nothingness of wild clouds in a blue sky and not a living thing in sight except the gophers. To the east and north and south there was no tree to break the line of the prairie, and to the west there was just a blue dimness that hid the rebellious foothills of the Rockies.

Then quite suddenly came Cheyenne, an overgrown small town perched like a lonely bird in the middle of these immense plains. And after all the quiet and expanse there was suddenly an airport, with a transcontinental plane skimming over it about to land, a Union Pacific Railroad Station with a great coloured sign over it, a domed State Capitol, a Main Street with flickering movies, cafés, shops, hotels with elevators, five- and ten-cent stores, modern clothes in windows, and an air of complete urbanity and sophistication.

The streets were full of people in summer clothing looking very unlonely and self-contained. There they were, a little busy colony hardly aware of the wilderness around them.

We had tea and went to a movie. On the middle of it I thought again of the brightness of the electric lights and signs outside, the noise of the cars and trains and elevators and aeroplanes; and just beyond, the deathly silence of that magnificent prairie.

This is the country of the frontier days, of covered wagons and stockades, of wild west movies and shrieking Indians, of Buffalo Bill, Deadwood Dick and Calamity Jane, of Wind River, Ten Sleep, Big Horn and Lost Cabin.

Some of the cities now sprouting a tentative sky-scraper in the down town business section are just fifty years old. Some of the London suburbs were villages in 1066. Rapid City, South Dakota, was, only fifty years ago, the bare edge of a wild and empty prairie, the home of gophers, wolves, buffaloes and deer.

The gophers are still there, millions of them. They dart across the road and sit up, paws neatly folded, as you pass. One day, following a car, I saw a pretty and lively one enjoying the sand and the sunshine and then—a huge rubber wheel—and it rolled over on its back, blood staining its white furry chest. The ones that escape sit up and look with surprise and interest at the Fords and Chevrolets and Plymouths that trundle along the newly surfaced roads.

The wolves have retired to the lonelier places, into North Dakota and Canada, the buffaloes are in corrals, looking meagre and pathetic, and the deer are shot among the mountains by tourists in the summer season and by natives in the Fall.

The West is not what it was. But I, for one, will take it for what it is, together with the rest of America, and my reward will come when I can say:

"You should have seen America in the nineteen thirties. Those were the days."

INDEX

INDEX

Foreign Travelers in America
1810–1935

AN ARNO PRESS COLLECTION

Archer, William. **America To-Day**: Observations and Reflections. 1899.

Belloc, Hilaire. **The Contrast.** 1924.

[Boardman, James]. **America, and the Americans.** By a Citizen of the World. 1833.

Bose, Sudhindra. **Fifteen Years in America.** 1920.

Bretherton, C. H. **Midas, Or, The United States and the Future.** 1926.

Bridge, James Howard (Harold Brydges). **Uncle Sam at Home.** 1888.

Brown, Elijah (Alan Raleigh). **The Real America.** 1913.

Combe, George. **Notes on the United States Of North America During a Phrenological Visit in 1838-9-40.** 1841. 2 volumes in one.

D'Estournelles de Constant, Paul H. B. **America and Her Problems.** 1915.

Duhamel, Georges. **America the Menace:** Scenes from the Life of the Future. Translated by Charles Miner Thompson. 1931.

Feiler, Arthur. **America Seen Through German Eyes.** Translated by Margaret Leland Goldsmith. 1928.

Fidler, Isaac. **Observations on Professions, Literature, Manners, and Emigration, in the United States and Canada, Made During a Residence There in 1832.** 1833.

Fitzgerald, William G. (Ignatius Phayre). **Can America Last?** A Survey of the Emigrant Empire from the Wilderness to World-Power Together With Its Claim to "Sovereignty" in the Western Hemisphere from Pole to Pole. 1933.

Gibbs, Philip. **People of Destiny:** Americans As I Saw Them at Home and Abroad. 1920.

Graham, Stephen. **With Poor Immigrants to America.** 1914.

Griffin, Lepel Henry. **The Great Republic.** 1884.

Hall, Basil. **Travels in North America in the Years 1827 and 1828.** 1829. 3 volumes in one.

Hannay, James Owen (George A. Birmingham). **From Dublin to Chicago:** Some Notes on a Tour in America. 1914.

Hardy, Mary (McDowell) Duffus. **Through Cities and Prairie Lands:** Sketches of an American Tour. 1881.

Holmes, Isaac. **An Account of the United States of America,** Derived from Actual Observation, During a Residence of Four Years in That Républic, Including Original Communications. [1823].

Ilf, Ilya and Eugene Petrov. **Little Golden America:** Two Famous Soviet Humorists Survey These United States. Translated by Charles Malamuth. 1937.

Kerr, Lennox. **Back Door Guest.** 1930.

Kipling, Rudyard. **American Notes.** 1899.

Leng, John. **America in 1876:** Pencillings During a Tour in the Centennial Year, With a Chapter on the Aspects of American Life. 1877.

Longworth, Maria Theresa (Yelverton). **Teresina in America.** 1875. 2 volumes in one.

Low, A[lfred] Maurice. **America at Home.** [1908].

Marshall, W[alter] G[ore]. **Through America:** Or, Nine Months in the United States. 1881.

Mitchell, Ronald Elwy. **America:** A Practical Handbook. 1935.

Moehring, Eugene P. **Urban America and the Foreign Traveler, 1815-1855.** With Selected Documents on 19th-Century American Cities. 1974.

Muir, Ramsay. **America the Golden:** An Englishman's Notes and Comparisons. 1927.

Price, M[organ] Philips. **America After Sixty Years:** The Travel Diaries of Two Generations of Englishmen. 1936.

Sala, George Augustus. **America Revisited:** From the Bay of New York to the Gulf of Mexico and from Lake Michigan to the Pacific. 1883. 3rd edition. 2 volumes in one.

Saunders, William. **Through the Light Continent;** Or, the United States in 1877-8. 1879. 2nd edition.

Smith, Frederick [Edwin] (Lord Birkenhead). **My American Visit.** 1918.

Stuart, James. **Three Years in North America.** 1833. 2 volumes in one.

Teeling, William. **American Stew.** 1933.

Vivian, H. Hussey. **Notes of a Tour in America from August 7th to November 17th, 1877.** 1878.

Wagner, Charles. **My Impressions of America.** Translated by Mary Louise Hendee. 1906.

Wells, H. G. **The Future in America:** A Search After Realities. 1906.